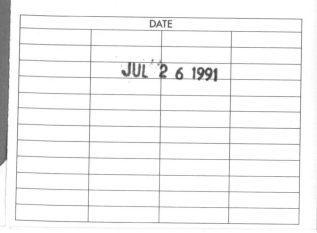

Counseling
Families
of Children
with Disabilities

RESOURCES FOR
CHRISTIAN COUNSELING

RESOURCES FOR CHRISTIAN COUNSELING

VOLUME TWENTY-FIVE

Counseling Families of Children with Disabilities

ROSEMARIE S. COOK, Ph.D.

RESOURCES FOR CHRISTIAN COUNSELING

—————— General Editor ——————

Gary R. Collins, Ph.D.

WORD PUBLISHING
Dallas · London · Vancouver · Melbourne

To Christopher Guy Cook,
who, as did the child Jesus,
continues to progress "steadily
in wisdom and age and grace
before God and men."
(Luke 2:52)

COUNSELING FAMILIES OF CHILDREN WITH DISABILITIES, Volume 25 of the Resources for Christian Counseling series. Copyright © 1990 by Word, Incorporated. All rights reserved. No portion of this book may be reproduced in any form, except for brief quotations in reviews, without written permission from the publisher.

Unless otherwise indicated, all Scripture quotations in this volume are from The New International Version, copyright © 1983 by the International Bible Society. Used by permission of Zondervan Bible Publishers. Scripture references indicated by KJV are from the King James Version; those identified as NAB are from the St. Joseph's Edition of the New American Bible, Catholic Book Publishing Company, New York, © 1970.

Library of Congress Cataloging-in-Publication Data

Cook, Rosemarie S., 1943 –
    Counseling families of children with disabilities / Rosemarie S. Cook
        p. cm.—(Resources for Christian counseling: v. 26)
    Includes bibliographical references and index.
    ISBN 0-8499-0738-1
    1. Parents of handicapped children—Pastoral counseling of.
I. Title. II. Series
BV4438.C66   1990
259'.4—dc20   90-45837
                                                                CIP

Printed in the United States of America

012349 AGF 987654321

CONTENTS

EDITOR'S PREFACE

I DON'T KNOW WHAT LED TO SHIRLEY'S DEATH. She was born on the same October day that I was born and her parents brought her, as my parents brought me, to the same neighborhood, on the same block of Wood Street.

When the time came to have childhood birthday parties, our mothers were surprised to discover they had two parties scheduled for the same time—with the same guest list. To avoid confusion, the mothers always coordinated their efforts in later years. As I recall, we took turns. One year Shirley's party would be on the exact date and mine would be a day late; the next year we would shift.

As Shirley got older, everybody noticed that she wasn't like the other neighborhood kids who came to her birthday party. She couldn't run and play like the rest of us, and eventually her weakened body was confined to a wheel chair. Shirley's parents must have watched with great anguish as their daughter's condition grew progressively worse. She died while she was still a teen-ager—like her older sister had died a few years before.

Many years have passed since Shirley's death, but I wonder if her parents struggled, like Rosemarie Cook struggled, with the discovery that a child was not developing like other children. Perhaps Shirley's parents faced the stares, the misunderstandings, the frustrations, the painful decisions, and the stresses that Dr. Cook faced as she raised her son. I suspect that Shirley's parents didn't have the faith, the knowledge, the understanding or the help that parents like Rosemarie Cook have today. But even if they could have been better informed, Shirley's parents would still have found pressure and personal pain in the midst of their challenge of raising a child with a disability.

As general editor of this book series, I am especially pleased that Dr. Cook's significant volume appears only a few weeks after President George Bush signed into law the Americans with Disabilities Act. Too often, as the following pages show, people with physical and mental disabilities face discrimination and frustration. So do their parents and siblings. Those of us who are not disabled sometimes feel uncomfortable counseling these people and maybe our discomforts add to their frustrations. Perhaps, too, our discomforts come because we lack understanding and knowledge of the struggles and special issues that are faced by people with disabilities and their families.

In the pages of this book, Dr. Rosemarie Cook helps to remove misunderstandings and increase our knowledge. Drawing on her professional expertise and her personal experiences, she brings to this book the perspectives of an educator, a counselor, and the mother of a son with a disability. Her book is informative, practical, and readable.

In each of the preceding volumes in the Resources for Christian Counseling series, I have tried to make a statement about the purposes of these blue and silver books. When we began, we were looking for authors who had a strong Christian commitment, impeccable counseling credentials, and extensive counseling experience. We wanted each of the books to be practical and helpful examples of accurate psychology and careful use of Scripture. Each was intended to have a clear evangelical perspective, careful documentation, a strong practical orientation, and freedom from the sweeping statements and undocumented rhetoric that sometimes characterize writing in the counseling field. Our goal was to provide books that would be clearly written, useful, up-to-date overviews of the issues faced by contemporary Christian counselors—including pastoral counselors. We agreed at the beginning that all of the Resources for Christian

Counseling books would have similar bindings and we hoped that together they would comprise a helpful encyclopedia of Christian counseling.

Now that we have published twenty-five volumes and are moving to the final volumes in the series, we have no reason to abandon our earlier goals. Looking back, I think two or three of the books have not lived up to our expectations as much as we had hoped. But most, including this volume by Rosemarie Cook, have been well produced, carefully documented, and practical. Already the books have proven to be helpful to many of us who are counselors.

Maybe you never had a Shirley on your street, like I did.

Maybe you are not often involved in counseling parents who have children with disabilities.

But your effectiveness as a Christian people-helper is likely to be increased as you ponder the message of the following pages. After reading this book I came away feeling better educated, challenged, and with a greater sense of compassion for the struggles of people with disabilities and their families. I suspect you will feel the same.

Gary R. Collins, Ph.D.
Kildeer, Illinois

INTRODUCTION

I HAVE, IN A SENSE, been preparing to write this book for twenty-five years, from the day that my son Christopher was born. I have dedicated this book to him because it was through daily living with him that I learned so much about the world of children with disabilities—as well as a lot about myself. I had other experiences with children with disabilities, both before and after Chris was born; but none of them could begin to approach the level of intensity that is inherent in being the parent of a child with disabilities.

Early in his life we suspected that there was a problem with Chris, but doctors did not want to listen to my concerns. To them, I was just another "worried mother." When Chris was three, we got the diagnosis from a female pediatrician who was not afraid to confront us with reality. This confirmed our fears, but also gave us permission to seek help. As strange as it may seem to those who have not endured such a challenge, we felt a great relief to have a name for this condition, as unwelcome as the label of mental retardation was. But from that point we could begin to discuss the problem and seek help.

Having a degree in education made it easier to learn the ropes in obtaining services for my child; but even then, I was often confused and frustrated. Then, when Chris was an adolescent, I became aware of forums where my voice could be heard, not only for my own child, but for other children with disabilities, too. These opportunities often came in conjunction with my work as a volunteer in organizations that serve children and adults with disabilities. I have performed this rewarding work for the last nine years.

The most important part of my story is the crisis point I reached with Chris, and how the Lord led me through that crisis into a new way of living. Since Chris's father was in the navy, he was away about one-third of Chris's growing-up years. A military wife often is, in essence, a single parent. In our household, concerns with the children's education became my role.

When Chris was ten years old, my husband, then a naval aviator, was away on a long cruise. The summer was one of loneliness, turmoil, and despair for me, alone with our four boys ages eleven, ten, five, and two. My usually sufficient self-reliance was not working, and I was near the end of my resources in dealing with all the boys, particularly with Chris.

Then another navy wife invited me to a ship's wives' Bible study, and a friend asked me to a weekly prayer meeting. In those sessions, I came to realize that I had not been making an attempt to listen to God, but just muddling through on my own. Through the ministries of these two wonderful groups of people, I learned that the words of the Bible were really for me, for today. I also learned what it meant to turn everything over to God and to listen for his voice.

Inner peace came when I rededicated myself to Jesus as Lord of my life. Part of that peace was from the realization that God loved my son even more than I did. My central fear had been that Chris would have no one to care for him if I became ill or died. But when I accepted God's boundless love, I received a gift of being able to trust that he would always provide for Chris in any circumstance. And I became convinced that he would do the same for me, as well—no matter what. Suddenly I knew I could make it, even though a few months earlier I had doubted my own ability to remain sane.

I wish I could tell you that Chris became a Phi Beta Kappa and there were marvelous signs and wonders in our lives. There was, instead, an ability to continue on with life, to continue caring for each other, and to continue living in the security that God is in control. There have been sunny days and rainy days and occasional hurricanes, but God's love has never failed.

Chris is now in a residential vocational program where staff members comment on his sense of peace and self-confidence, and the joy he brings to others.

Having traveled this road for many years, I have wanted to reach out to other families who may be struggling along its ups and downs. But I want to do more than just give information. Information is needed; but my desire is to help families in a manner that will enable them to tap into the abundant life promised in John 10:10. And I also want to help counselors enable these families to develop their own strengths and resources for coping with this life-long challenge.

Counselors should also feel encouraged to enthusiastically take a role in initiating the inclusion of children and adults with disabilities and their families into the life of the local church. Exclusion of those with disabilities from church activities and church ministries is not intentional, but it occurs because people are either unaware of needs or of the means to meet those needs. As pastors and counselors effectively help these families, they may participate in extending the support and outreach of the local church to them, both as follow-up and as prevention.

CHAPTER ONE
AN OVERVIEW OF DISABILITY

THE DEFINITION OF A DISABLED PERSON depends on the time and place in which one lives. In one sense, we are all disabled, or have the potential to be labeled as such. For example, I am nearsighted. Without corrective lenses, I would fit into the classic definition of one who has a developmental disability—a permanent condition developed before age eighteen that would significantly affect my ability to function.

The most common visual image that accompanies the word "disabled" is a wheelchair, the worldwide symbol for handicapped parking spaces and other accommodations. In reality, disability entails a wide range of conditions and includes both mental and physical impairment.

PEOPLE FIRST CONCEPT

Two separate concepts have influenced the choice of terminology in this book. The first is a "people first" orientation that involves speaking of the person first and then of the condition. We refer to "children with disabilities," not "the retarded" or "the epileptics." These latter terms speak of people as though they were equivalent to their labels or diagnoses.

Second, there is a difference between disability and handicap. A disability refers to a functional limitation that interferes with a person's ability to see, walk, hear, communicate or understand—functions which are inherent in the person. A handicap is a barrier or situation that is imposed by society, the environment, or oneself.[1]

This may seem a matter of semantics; but in the words of Ohio Governor Richard F. Celeste, "Words drive thought and thought drives action; if we use language that focuses on an individual as a person rather than a disability we will undoubtedly develop programs and provide services that help to maximize the independence, productivity and integration of persons with disabilities in our society."[2]

Referring to people in terms of labels or diagnoses puts them into groups about which we may have a bias or misperception. Thus, we study quadriplegics and forget that they are people who come in all shapes, sizes, colors, temperaments, educational backgrounds, faith experiences, vocations, and interests. The unique qualities of persons must never be forgotten in attempting to discover their commonalities.

The word *disability* rather than *handicap* is used throughout this book. Although neither the dictionary nor the thesaurus makes a definitive differentiation between the two, there is a subtle shade of difference in their modern usage.

A person with a *disability* becomes *handicapped* because of an environment which does not provide adaptation and accommodation. Without corrective lenses and hearing aids, many of us would be handicapped. Without a wheelchair, the person who cannot walk becomes handicapped. Without electric doors, curb cuts, or buses with lifts, the person in the wheelchair is handicapped again. Without a loving and accepting community, the person with a physical or mental disability is truly handicapped.

RATIONALE FOR COUNSELING

As counselors, we may not be aware of what constitutes a disability or of the needs for our services in this area. Part of the problem is that no singular definition of disability exists. The dictionary definition is ". . . the inability to pursue an occupation because of physical or mental impairment; lack of legal qualifications to do something; a nonlegal disqualification, restriction or disadvantage."[3] But other definitions also must be considered.

Governmental Definitions

In the United States the federal government has several definitions of disability. One set of definitions refers to specific classifications for children who are served under Public Law 94–142, the Education for All Handicapped Children Act of 1975. Other definitions exist for individuals' entitlements under programs such as SSI (Supplemental Security Income) or their eligibility for programs such as workman's compensation or Medicaid. Local, state, or federal agencies often use separate terms to define eligibility for their services to the developmentally disabled, the physically disabled, and the psychiatrically disabled.

Psychological Definitions

A further ambiguity in definition becomes apparent when we consult the *DSM-III-R (Diagnostic and Statistical Review, Third Edition, Revised).*[4] Developmental disorders, coded on Axis II, are listed under the main headings of Mental Retardation, Pervasive Developmental Disorders, Specific Developmental Disorders, and Other Developmental Disorders. Virtually all of these disorders would classify children as eligible for special education under PL 94–142, but the names of the disorders do not always correspond to the federal classifications for special education. ". . . There is, from a psychological point of view, no true definition of handicap and no definitive cut-off."[5]

In addition, some *DSM-III-R* classifications listed under "Disorders First Evident in Infancy, Childhood and Adolescence"[6] would include a child in special education and others would not. For example, under "Disruptive Behavior Disorders,"[7] a child diagnosed with attention-deficit hyperactivity disorder may or may not be included in special education, depending upon the degree of behavior disturbance and/or any accompanying learning disabilities.

Placement of a child in special education varies from school district to school district, and there may even be differences among schools in the same district, depending upon the autonomy of the school principal and other existing policies. Although the law is a federal one, enforcement varies widely despite state and federal reviews. In addition, the official documentation of the school district may not show what actually occurs in practice; even though the letter of the law may be met, the spirit of the law does not necessarily occur.

Developmental Disabilities

The term *developmental disabilities* is applied to a broad spectrum of conditions and disorders that impair intellectual and/or physical functioning in a person and that require adaptive behavior. This includes, among many other conditions, mental retardation, cerebral palsy, epilepsy, learning disabilities, autism, or functioning that is impaired through disease or accident. Developmental disability is generally used in legislation, agency services, advocacy, and to some extent in education. It includes these main concepts:

- a disability that originated before or during early adulthood (variously defined as either age eighteen or twenty-one)
- a condition that is permanent or is expected to continue indefinitely, and
- a disability that is ". . . a substantial impediment to the person's ability to function independently and normally in society."[8]

The focus of this book is on families whose children developed problems before or during birth, or as children or teen-agers. Although counselors may have a concern for all families who have a loved one with a disability, we must set limits on the information provided in this book to prevent it from becoming encyclopedic. Many people are struggling to cope with an adult who has become disabled through trauma or disease. There are also many elderly persons who have become limited in activity. We would certainly include both of these groups in pleas made for awareness, understanding, and services.

Some issues are common to all families that have a loved one with a limitation or a disability; but families who have children with developmental disabilities have specific concerns that need to be addressed in a separate format. For example, there is a different focus when a parent becomes disabled because of a car accident than when a similar occurrence involves a child. An adult developing multiple sclerosis presents different challenges to family life than a child with cerebral palsy.

Each of these disabilities calls for a unique set of counseling issues. And while the apostle Paul may have had the ability to be "all things to all men" an attempt to do that in this book would result in ineffectiveness to all.

SUMMARY OF AVAILABLE DATA

The exact number of families affected by a developmental disability is unknown for several reasons. The first problem relates to definition, as discussed earlier. Being able to collect universal and systematic data requires an operational definition of disability and a clear statement of purpose. But people are not neatly divided into disabled and nondisabled categories. And it is sometimes difficult to determine at what point a disability becomes a handicap. Some persons who are classified as disabled would not also be considered handicapped. Limited ability to perform a major life activity as the direct result of an impairment is central to the notion of disability.[9]

Second, regular and systematic data on those with disabilities does not exist. The multitude of sources of data are fragmented. Many researchers and agencies collect data but with differing intentions, criteria, and classification systems. This array of information regarding persons with disabilities is confusing and those researching practical statistics often find themselves comparing two different sets of numbers.[10] Also, data may not be current because of an extensive time lapse between collection and publication.

The National Center for Health Statistics conducted a National Health Interview Survey and showed that ". . . over 31 million persons or 14.6 percent of the population reported some degree of chronic activity limitation."[11] A "chronic activity limitation" was defined as a restriction in activity as a result of a condition which began at least three months prior; it was also defined as a condition that is always considered chronic—for example, the loss of a limb.

The National Center for Health Statistics recently reported that 90.4 percent of America's 1.3 million nursing-home residents were

5

dependent for help with daily living activities.[12] Other recent data showed that there were 119,000 residents living in state residential institutions for the mentally retarded.[13] This does not include those in community residential settings, or those living with their families or in foster care. The prevalence rate of mental retardation remains at about 3 percent of the population, according to the Association of Retarded Citizens (ARC),[14] and the *DSM-III-R* lists it at 1 percent.[15] The ARC also states that one out of every ten Americans has a person with mental retardation in his or her extended family.[16]

Incidence and Prevalence

The terms *incidence* and *prevalence* are often used interchangeably, but they are actually different—a nuance of statistical reporting that has implications when discussing an issue. *Incidence* is the number of new cases within a given period of time, usually in a calendar year. *Prevalence* is the existing number of cases at a given point in time. For example, the number of babies born with Down's syndrome in a given year is the incidence; the number of persons who have Down's syndrome in 1990 is the prevalence. These numbers may be expressed in actual numbers or may be given as a percentage of the total population or the total number of those with disabilities.

The need for incidence and prevalence rates exists to justify programs or validate the significance of a problem, particularly to obtain funding. These statistics also are necessary in monitoring and administering of public health, but are of no practical help in day-to-day life.

Definition by Attitudes

Awareness of the numbers is important; but it is more important to be attuned to attitudes and individual needs. Jim Abbott, a baseball pitcher for the California Angels, has no right hand, but he hurls a fastball clocked at ninety-four miles per hour. He was one of relatively few major-league players to be signed on with no minor-league experience. Does he have a disability, a handicap, or a chronic activity limitation?

A young man I know, Gregory S., has no physical problems that limit activity, but he is considered disabled because of mental retardation. If Gregory were living on a farm, and if education were not compulsory, perhaps there would be no label. He would just do the work that he is able to do and would be considered a functional member of the family and the community. Certainly people would notice his differences, but it is possible that he would be more accepted and assimilated into a rural community than is possible in a more modern, urban setting.

In the Camphill[17] and L'Arche[18] communities, there is no need for labels, for all residents live together in community, both those who have disabilities and those who do not. Although these communities were founded along differing philosophical or religious orientations, they have some similarities, including the goals of promoting the growth of each person in the community and celebrating the giftedness of all. Conceived after World War II, these types of communities are currently more extensively developed in Europe than in the United States. They will be described in more detail in chapter 7.

Community is hardly a new term to Christians, for we have several models in both the Old and New Testaments of how we are called to minister to one another in community. Acts 4:32–35 presents one example. In contrast, the world labels those with disabilities and separates them out. The resulting programs constantly compete for funding in order to function, while lacking mechanisms of cooperation that would allow them to serve their common populations more effectively.

Christians, however, recognize that we are all part of the body of Christ, with all members not only equally worthy of attention, but also equally having a functioning part in the body, as explained in Romans 12. If there is a function for all then there is also an obligation to care for all. Paul wrote eloquently to the Ephesians on this subject, stating that we are to be patient and to bear with one another in love, as parts of this one body in one Lord.

Mephibosheth, grandson of Saul and son of Jonathan, was crippled in both feet. (In some translations, he is called Meribbaal.) Mephibosheth referred to himself as a "dead dog," yet David placed him at a position of honor at the king's table, "like one of the king's sons" (2 Sam. 9:11). In biblical times, people with physical impairments were often reduced to begging for their existence. David did more than provide daily bread and shelter for Mephibosheth; he raised him to a high position in the household because of his lineage. Similarly, we are highly positioned, too, as heirs to the kingdom of heaven, despite the condition of our bodies. And like David, we, too, should be concerned with raising others to places of honor because of our shared lineage in Jesus Christ.

COUNSELING IMPLICATIONS

A pastor or counselor may feel inadequate to counsel a family because he or she lacks knowledge of specific disability conditions. But a counselor does not have to be an expert on disorders to be an effective helper. Instead, we need a working knowledge of the condition, and this can come through the many available information resources. Appendix II of this book includes a list of disability-related organizations; virtually all of these have materials which are available free or at little cost. Several excellent reference books are also listed.

Effective counselors will use the same types of proven counseling skills with families who have children with disabilities as they would with any family; but in dealing with a disability, they also will focus on the following areas:

- What abilities does the child possess?
- What are the unique needs of this child?
- What are the family's strengths, resources, and capabilities?
- What are the unique needs of this family?
- How can we, in the body of Christ, minister to the needs of the child and of the family?
- Who else, in the church and in the community, can be of help to this family?
- What can the counselor or pastor do to develop missing resources in the church and in the community?

Throughout this book, these issues are addressed at various stages of development of both the child and the family.

MYTHS AND STEREOTYPES

All of us, including counselors, carry around an arsenal of pat answers and myths that categorize information and let us make sense of the universe so we can go on about our daily lives without too much thought. While this lets us avoid trivializing our lives in some ways, it also creates common items of misinformation. The following questions and statements may dispel some of the current misinformation regarding disabilities:

1. *What is the most common lethal, inherited disorder among Caucasians?*

Researchers asking this question in a major American city found no one who could give the correct answer, which is cystic fibrosis. Although many of the people surveyed had contributed to the Cystic Fibrosis Foundation, they were not aware that the occurrence at birth of cystic fibrosis was one in sixteen hundred for the Caucasian population in the United States, giving this disorder its top ranking.[19]

2. *Under which classifications are most of the children in special education in the United States placed?*

Special education is not only for children in wheelchairs and those who are mentally retarded. The largest classification of children in special education are those with learning disabilities and those who receive speech therapy. Approximately 70 percent of all children in special education are in these two categories.[20]

3. *Is a learning disability a permanent disability, or is it just a temporary learning problem that can be cured?*

A learning disability may be the last diagnosis most people would list as a disabling condition, but it is a very real disability to millions of people. It is often a hidden disability, one that if diagnosed at all, is rarely known before the child enters school.

Many people go through life wondering what is wrong with themselves, working hard at learning tasks that others seem to accomplish without nearly as much effort. They are adults with undiagnosed learning disabilities who experience frustration in learning and have suffered from accompanying low self-esteem for much of their lives. Some graduate students did not realize that they were struggling with learning disabilities until they were in their thirties or forties.

There is no cure for learning disabilities, but there is accommodation and compensation. That is why it is essential that children be diagnosed and remediation be started as early as possible. Then essential learning is not missed and a child's positive self-concept can be continually enhanced.

4. *How is a person's IQ score related to his or her functioning?*

Those who are classified as mentally retarded are grouped into four IQ score categories for diagnostic and educational purposes.

Of the 2.5 to 3 percent of the American population that are classified as retarded, over 85 percent have IQ scores ranging from 55 to 69 and are called mildly retarded.[21] The *DSM-III-R* states that these people can attain about a sixth-grade level of education; and unless there is an additional problem, they can successfully live in the community independently, or in supervised apartments or in group homes.[22]

Those who score between 35–40 and 50–55 are called moderately retarded and comprise about 10 percent of all those who are retarded. They can attain about a second-grade level of education, and are able to live in supervised group homes in the community.[23]

Those who score between 20–25 to 35–40 are classified as severely retarded and comprise about 3 to 4 percent of all of those who are retarded. They can learn "survival" words by sight, may perform simple tasks with supervision, and can live in the community. Some may have an associated handicap and require additional nursing care.[24]

From 1 to 2 percent of the population called retarded are classified as severe with IQ scores below 20–25. These people live in various settings ranging from the community to intermediate- or skilled-care facilities. They can attend day programs for leisure and recreation.[25]

The overlap of IQ scores used in diagnosis shows that reliance on score alone is an oversimplification. Diagnosis should never be made on the basis of IQ alone. Although many counselors are not psychometricians, it is crucial for them to be at least familiar with the terminology and the classification systems when helping parents. Parents also need this information to understand their own child's disability and to deal with issues that center around school and later life planning.

5. *Where is care provided for children and adults with disabilities?*

Most children and adults with disabilities are living with and are cared for by their parents or other relatives. The move toward deinstitutionalization and normalization that began in the 1960s continues today, still influenced by the civil rights movement and the philosophy that those with disabilities also have equal rights under the law. These rights include the right to live in their own communities and the right to live as normal a life as possible, in the least restrictive environment in which they are capable of functioning.

Relatively few people with disabilities are now placed in institutions, in part because the institutions have fewer beds available, and also because families do not want their loved ones there. Also, education for all children under PL 94–142 now means that children with disabilities can live in their own homes and attend local schools.

As these trends continue, the social stigma of having a child with a mental or physical disability has diminished. Although we have not yet achieved society's total acceptance of people with disabilities, we no longer keep our children out of sight or entrust them to others for lifelong care from birth. We must remember, however, that not all children can or should be cared for in the home—there are children whose needs are so extensive that the best solution is for the family to seek residential placement. However, families facing this decision now have a variety of options that did not exist several years ago.

My own experience twenty years ago was being told by a physician to place my child with a disability in an institution and then to concentrate on the one other child I had at the time. I chose not to follow that advice, and today, that child I was supposed to forget can read on a first-grade level, tend to his own self-care needs, and perform a variety of work skills.

There are many implications for counselors and churches regarding those families whose children with disabilities are living at home. The challenge for the church may be to locate these families, welcome them into the congregation, and then to enable them to participate in the life of the church.

CHAPTER TWO

THE FIVE-FACTOR MODEL OF FAMILY STRESS AND CRISIS

A FAMILY IS A DYNAMIC, vital, ever-changing entity. It can never actually be the same, even for two days in a row, as its members leave the house, interact with others, and then return and interact with each other in a manner that reflects those outside experiences. The paradox is that, although individuals change, the family constantly struggles to keep patterns of interaction constant throughout the years. For example, the rituals and celebrations of family life, both formal and informal, often remain unchanged through the years, as though the specific content of each ritual may be ever-changing, but the process, itself, remains constant.

The family as an entity is reluctant to change; it wants to maintain balance and stability while its individual members are growing and changing according to their separate developmental schedules. Those changes are constantly occurring in the physical, emotional, spiritual, and intellectual spheres for each person; subsequently, the collective family as a whole changes, too.

STAGES OF THE FAMILY LIFE SPAN

Some changes in families and in individuals are predictable and expected. Newlyweds are in one stage of their marriage and probably have some definite expectations of what life will be like as a couple five and ten years later. When a child is born, there are expectations about growth and development, as well as the normal school progression.

In contrast, families also experience unplanned events such as illness, accident, or untimely death which are both significant and unpredictable. John Lennon was not far wrong when he said that "life is what happens while you are making other plans."[1]

Families are comfortable when development of individual members is "on schedule" and when the family seems to be moving along as expected. Events that interfere with the normal expected cycles of life, often viewed as crises, throw the family out of balance.

CRITICAL TRANSITIONS IN FAMILY LIFE

Evelyn Duvall and Reuben Hill identified eight critical transitions in family life, each leading to a new stage of development with individual and family tasks to be mastered at each stage.[2] These are:

1. *Newly married, becoming a couple*—disengaging from the role of son or daughter, sister or brother; leaving the parental home; leaving school; taking on the role of being a husband or wife; taking on the role of an in-law; changing the friendship network.

2. *First parenthood*—family dyad becomes a triad; taking on the role of mother or father; expanding the residence to accommodate an infant; becoming reconnected with the extended family network; mother may leave the labor force.

3. *Transactional relations with schools and neighbors*—oldest child enters school; youngest child is born; need for a larger house to accommodate growing family may result in first purchase of a home; becoming more cohesive as a family.

4. *Dual-earner family, disengagement of children*—the oldest child will shift to closer identification with peers than with family; youngest

child enters school; mother may enter work force or school; family's debt and financial obligations may increase.

5. *Launching children*—the oldest child leaves school, enters work force, marries, leaves home; youngest child more closely identifies with peers than with family; parents become in-laws; family may interact with different groups as children leave home.

6. *Middle-age marriage and grandparenthood*—moving to a smaller house or apartment; return to a dyad; retiring from being parents, taking on the roles of grandparents.

7. *Retirement and aging*—retiring from the labor force; status and leadership role losses; reduction of many of life's roles; possible move to a nursing home.

This model, developed in 1948, is considered a classic in the field of family stress and crisis theory. Although it has general application today, it cannot accommodate all of the current variations in family life, including single-parent families, stepfamilies, women who have careers and then children, women who work throughout marriage, and the longer, more fulfilling life of senior citizens. Despite these modern variations, though, what remains consistent and applicable to all types of families with children is the child's progression within the family from dependence to ever-increasing independence, finally exiting the home of origin to establish life as an independent adult.

DEFINITION OF CRISIS

We can all name the stressors in our lives—the people, the situations, and the events that cause us to feel pain and pleasure. Each contribute to our sense of well-being as well as our feelings of fear, distrust, confusion, and unworthiness.

A general definition of crisis is ". . . a perception of an event or situation as an intolerable difficulty that exceeds the resources and coping mechanisms of the person"[3] or, in our case, of the family. Two types of crises affect a family: developmental crises precipitated by biology or social progression (such as puberty or retirement), and situational crises from non-normative events (such as a house fire or death in an auto accident).[4]

Certain elements inherent in an event signify a crisis situation as a multidimensional event. The factors that define crisis are presented in Figure 2–1.

Significant Factors in Crisis

---

1. An imbalance between the difficulty and importance of the problem, and the coping resources and problem-solving skills of the family.[5]

2. Extreme distress if the family denies or avoids the problem.[6]

3. Failure of normal resources and mechanisms to resolve the problem.[7]

4. A family determination that the problem is a crisis.[8]

5. A family history of failure in problem resolution.[9]

6. A repeating cycle of applying known problem solutions that produce failure and additional tension until homeostatic balance is lost.[10]

7. A time period of one to six weeks.[11] During that time the crisis is resolved for better or for worse (breakdown) or shoved aside, only to erupt again at some other point.[12]

8. Long-term and short-term implications.

9. Elements of opportunity for growth; the challenge may bring out new coping mechanisms and strengths.[13]

10. Elements of either a threat, a loss, or a challenge.[14]

11. Anxiety is always present, and serves as an impetus for change.[15]

12. Requires the family to use outside resources.[16]

13. Resolution may require that the family "freeze out" the deviant family member who is perceived as causing the crisis.[17]

Figure 2–1

CRISIS AND DISABILITY

No model of family development, stress, and crisis fully describes the family of a child with a disability. The factors in Figure 2–1 are applicable to both situational and developmental crises. Situational crises affect all families equally. However, the element of disability places a family in a unique and somewhat precarious position to be vulnerable to developmental crises.

All families with children will have stages generally following the progression described earlier. Most of these stages will be focused on the children. Critical transition points, such as graduation from high school, are generally predictable for families. But each critical transition has the potential to affect families differently, depending on whether the transition is considered as normal, stressful, or a crisis. Disability is an additional factor that works in concert with other events to determine whether a critical transition becomes a crisis.

Having a child with a disability upsets expectations of future stages for the family, which finds that making plans for the future becomes more complex as the child grows older. The stages for this family are different than those of other families because:

- There is extended or permanent dependence.
- Normal peer involvement of the child does not exist.
- The family's interaction with the community becomes much more widespread at an earlier stage and in a more intense manner.
- Parental planning will be restricted by more limits on personal freedom, disposable income, choice of recreation, where to reside, what job to take, or perhaps even whether to work.

The critical transitions of the child who has a disability have significant potential for becoming crises. Events such as the beginning of school, reaching puberty, or leaving the school system signify that some change will also occur in the workings of the family. Living patterns will be affected; perhaps the family will have to find additional resources. Choices may be limited, preventing the family from reaching what it considers a "best" solution to the problem, and resulting in frustration and further stress.

In addition, the critical transitions of launching other siblings may have more than the usual implications for the family if leaving home affects the physical, social, or emotional needs of the child with a disability. Again, a normal event accompanied by an additional stressor can propel the family into crisis.

The factor that is most significant, however, is that disability is permanent and lifelong, and will be superimposed in some way on each family member forever. The situation will always be there, with the family never being totally free of having to problem-solve around this one member. Problems will be a constant situation for this family; only the names of the problems will change.

Escalation of Stressors

A wedding provides an illustration of how stressors can easily escalate a normal event into a crisis for the family of a child with a disability. Let's suppose Bill Rush and Jan Dare are being married. Bill has a fifteen-year-old brother, David, who has cerebral palsy. The family is facing a decision of whether or not David should attend the wedding, because of concerns about his possible behavior during the wedding and reception, such as speaking out loud at inappropriate times.

Bill and Jan have discussed David's attendance at the wedding many times and have decided to leave the decision to Bill's parents. If the decision is yes, then someone will have to be named to spend the day with David, keep him quiet at the church, and tend to his needs at the reception. If the decision is no, then David will be missed, there will be a definite void, and the family will feel incomplete at what should be an event for all its members to share. Bill's parents are reminded more than ever that they will probably never attend a wedding for David, and their roles as lifelong caretakers seem to be more significant than ever.

If Mr. and Mrs. Rush disagree with each other about David's attendance, if their marriage has problems, and if the problem of David's attendance is not resolved in a manner that is mutually satisfactory, all of this can become fuel for additional arguments later. If Mr. Rush insists David attend and Mrs. Rush does not agree, and then if David does indeed call out "Hi, Bill!" in the middle of the "I do's," a major marital argument could ensue.

It may seem insignificant to others, and no one will ever do a research study on "Attendance at Weddings of Nondisabled Siblings by Disabled Siblings," but if this is your family, this is significant. What might seem like a minor problem takes on out-of-proportion significance in this family's course of events. It is an illustration of how differently the family of a child with a disability must cope, what added resources and strengths are needed, and what additional stressors can be present.

A MODEL FOR COUNSELING

Volumes have been written on family stress and crisis, and the search continues to clearly define contributing variables. For example, Klein and Hill listed fifty-eight variables developed by Joan Aldous in her research on family problem-solving; then they presented twenty propositions that summarized the effects of interaction variables on family problem-solving effectiveness.[18] The challenge now is to develop a workable model with practical application to disability for the counselor to use with the family. I believe the Five-Factor Model of Family Stress and Crisis will provide that practicality. The Five-Factor Model is the basis of the Annotated Family Appraisal, referred to throughout this book as the AFA, which is found in Appendix I.

The model was developed from studying the research results of many theorists in the field of family stress and crisis and then formulating the most salient and applicable components into an instrument for the counselor's use.

Implications of Family Stages

Mederer and Hill's critical transitions of family life are very child-centered. In general, they describe the growth and development of the children, and particularly the age of the youngest child, as driving the states of the family. Parental interactions with extended family members, neighbors, and community organizations vary according to the ages and needs of the children. Parental employment, leisure time, and choice of housing are usually based on the children's needs. Families make plans, financial and otherwise, based on assumptions about expected occurrences that most often center around children.

Counselors recognize that each family and each person in the family has a unique story to tell. Despite this uniqueness, humans, like families, share a commonality of progression through the stages of individual life, traversing on a birth-to-death-to-eternal-life continuum, largely experiencing universal events.

Although it is possible for each of us to look at ourselves five or ten years ago and recognize that we are in a different stage of our lives now than we were then, it is often unclear at what point we moved from one stage to another. There are marker events, to be sure, such as the birth or death of a family member; but even events that are fixed in time do not tell us when we entered a new stage. For example, when a woman is pregnant with the last child of the family, the family's changes begin with the pregnancy's announcement. Further changes occur as the pregnancy progresses and when the child is born. The critical transition of the last child's birth actually occurs over a number of months—not on a single day.

The Need for a Working Model

The counselor involved with the family of a child with a disability may be inclined to make broad assumptions about the family based on some basic perceptions about disabilities gathered along the way. That attitude is a disservice, because it fails to take into account the uniqueness of each family.

For example, the death of a parent has the potential to affect two siblings in a family in very different ways. One sibling may see it as a challenge to achieve goals, while another may give up on goals as a result of the parent's death.

Many hypotheses attempt to explain why persons differ in their reactions to stressors. For example, the Holmes and Rahe life events scale, developed in 1967 and now found in many texts and popular works, demonstrates the "victim" hypothesis. It predicts that emotional and physical exhaustion and concomitant health problems will result within a year or two after a number of circumstances have happened to a person over which that person has no control.[19]

The "vulnerability hypothesis" is based on the assumption that a person may suffer adverse health outcomes because of being more vulnerable to the impact of life events, existing personal disposition, and social conditions.[20]

The "proneness hypothesis" suggests that an existing disorder leads to a high frequency of negative life events, which then lead to further disorders.[21]

The "additive burden" and "chronic burden" hypotheses are variations of each other. The additive idea is that personal and environmental factors add to the stress of life events. The chronic concept is related to proneness, but is more causative, in that the existing disorder leads to a high frequency of negative life events, which lead to further disorder.[22]

None of these hypotheses has been supported by strong statistical indicators.

Additional research has shown the influence of "hassles" in contributing to a crisis. Hassles are everyday stressors that contribute to emotional and/or physical disorders. According to this research, these smaller, more proximal events in our lives are to be considered in the assessing of the impact of major life events on an individual.[23]

We commonly believe that social support is a positive mediating factor in a crisis. This concept is foundational to the widespread use of self-help groups. However, neither the concept of hassles nor of social support is strongly supported by research, due to difficulties in measurement techniques for both.[24]

THE FIVE-FACTOR MODEL OF FAMILY STRESS AND CRISIS

There appears to be no one singular explanation for the phenomenon of crisis. A more likely hypothesis is that crises result from an interaction of factors; the Five-Factor Model is based on that assumption. The components of the model provide a framework for the Annotated Family Appraisal (AFA), which gives the counselor a practical tool for assessment, treatment, and prevention of crisis.

The model is presented as a rectangular arrangement of elements in rows and columns. This is called a matrix. As you can see from Figure 2–2, the basic factors for the AFA are arranged in a matrix which suggests their interaction.[25] It is within this matrix that we can understand how stressors and problems can develop into a crisis. It is also within this matrix that the possibility of problem-solving and healing exists.

The first three components of the matrix are from Reuben Hill's ABCX model: the stressor event, A, the family's crisis-meeting resources, B, and the definition the family makes of the event, C.[26] According to Hill, A interacting with B interacting with C produces X, the crisis.

The next component in the model is that of a residual past, based on some elements of the Double ABCX model by McCubbin and Patterson.[27] The family's adaptation to past crises or problem

Five-Factor Model of Family Stress and Crisis

Stressor Event	Family's Resources	Family's Definition of Event	Family's Residual Past	Family's Readiness
Source —external —internal	Financial	View of situation as danger/opportunity	Past problem-solving experiences	Predictability
Dismemberment	Family adaptation	Rally against external cause	Unresolved conflicts from past crises	Expectedness
Accession	Family cohesion	Definition of God	Leftovers from compromises	Preparedness
Demoralization	Weakness/strengths of marital couple			
Status changes	Weakness/strengths of interpersonal relationships			
Role conflicts	External family resources			
Amount of change	Role agreement			
Suddenness	Faith			
Time span				

Figure 2–2

situations helps to determine what issues remain and what long-term consequences may now affect the present situation. The last component is "readiness," and addresses the family's current problem-solving skills in terms of its anticipation of problems from a cognitive-behavioral perspective.[28]

The following discussion explains each component of the model—the event, the family's resources, its definition of the event, its residual past, and its readiness—and elaborates on specific factors included in the AFA.

The Event

The first component of the model is the event itself. No one event will produce the same reaction in all families. The impact of an event has a range of possibilities, depending upon the number, intensity, and direction (positive or negative) of the changes that the event necessitates in the family's life.

The stressor event can be cataloged as to source, effect upon the family configuration, or type of event.[29]

The source of the event can be outside the family or from within the family. An external event is a political or natural occurrence such as a hurricane, a flood, or political or religious persecution. These events are outside of the family's control and have a potential to solidify the family as it works together to fight the stressor event or modify its effects.

In contrast, intra-family events have a potential for producing breakdown and disorganization in the family because they reflect upon problems inherent in family relationships. Examples of these events are infidelity, suicide, and alcoholism.

Many intra-family events can be distinguished further by the categories of dismemberment, accession, and demoralization. Dismemberment is the loss of a family member, accession is the unprepared-for addition of a family member, and demoralization is loss of morale and family unity. These may be permanent or temporary occurrences, and are related to the significantly realigned roles of family members as a result of the event.

Dismemberment can be the death of a family member, a parent being away for a number of months because of work or military duty, hospitalization of a family member, removal of a family member to a nursing home, or placing a family member with a disability outside the home.

Accession can be an unexpected, unwanted pregnancy, the return of someone who had deserted the family, the return of an adult child, addition of stepparents and stepsiblings, the addition of a son-in-law or daughter-in-law through an unexpected marriage, an elderly relative who comes to live with the family, or an extended family member, such as a niece or nephew, who comes to reside with the family.

Demoralization occurs when there is infidelity, alcoholism, substance abuse, or criminal activity that brings disgrace to the family. Demoralization also exists in conjunction with dismemberment or accession, as when a teen-ager in the family becomes pregnant, a child runs away, a spouse deserts the family, a divorce occurs, a family member is imprisoned, or a family member is institutionalized.

It is also important to take note of *status changes* and *role conflicts* in the family. Stressors that involve status shifts are situations such as a sudden loss of finances, a long period of unemployment, a sudden acquisition of wealth, suddenly becoming famous, a natural disaster, and becoming a refugee. Role conflict occurs as status changes, or because spousal or parental-child expectations differ.

Each of these classification systems has some variables related to the event itself. These are: the *amount of change* the crisis creates, the *suddenness* of the event, the *amount of time* the event is anticipated, the *length of time* that the family experiences disruptions, and the *long-term effects* on the family.

Family Resources

Hill's B factor is the crisis-meeting resources of the family.[30] The first, and often most obvious resource, is *financial*. The cost of caring for a child with a disability is not a problem for someone with several (or perhaps even one) million dollars; but it can be crucial to a low-income mother who is struggling to provide a thousand dollars to pay for a wheelchair for her child with cerebral palsy. These examples obviously represent extreme ends of the continuum of financial need and resources, with most people caught somewhere in the middle.

Other resources include the amount or lack of *family adaptation and cohesion,* the *rigidity* of the family and of individual *personality* structures, the weakness or strength of the interpersonal relationships of those *extended family members* who are sources of help to the family, and the availability and use of *resources outside the family.*

One variable of particular significance which can be weighted far more heavily than any other is the strength of the *marital dyad,* including the couple's capacity for intimacy. Chapter 8 explores this factor in greater detail.

In addition, for the family of a child with a disability, the resources include a host of sociological and environmental factors, including *community/school/church support.* These components should be considered in making decisions because they often provide services that the family cannot provide for itself.

Agreement of roles of the family members is another significant element that must be considered within this category of resources. When a child has special needs, his or her family members' roles can shift, and over time certain family members bear a much higher percentage of responsibility for care of the child than others. A detrimental pattern may be established, locking these people into caregiving roles which shut out the possibility for developing other areas of their lives.

The resource of *faith* also belongs in this row of the matrix. There are some studies that, in attempting to identify faith as a resource, list church membership or church attendance as variables. While both are usually components of having a faith, neither are indicators of faith. The most valid assessment of faith is from a subjective perspective—the meaning of faith to the individual. This is more fully explored in chapter 9.

A mature faith and trust in God is a resource in any crisis situation and should be considered in the assessment of a family's situation. The variance of faith in individual family members and how family functioning is affected by that variance should also be identified.

Family Definition of the Event

The third factor of Hill's model used in this matrix is the definition that the family makes of the crisis situation: What, subjectively, do the family members say this crisis means to them?[31] This factor reflects several facets of a family's personality. For example, do family members view the situation as a *challenge for growth,* reflecting the meaning of the Chinese character for crisis, which contains both danger and opportunity? Or do they define the event as a *problem they cannot solve?*

All members of the family may not view the crisis in the same light. Some members may assign *blame* for the event to others, either inside or outside of the family. If there are identifiable external causes, the family's responsibility and vulnerability are reduced. This allows them to join forces and rally against the external cause.

However in cases where there are no identifiable causes, which is usually true when a child has a disability, blame may be assigned or self-appropriated by immediate or extended family members. For example, a parent may view the child's condition as punishment for past sins and so take on the blame. Grandparents may blame the expectant mother's diet, her working up until time of delivery, or anything that they can construe which would help them make sense of the event.

Faith is also a consideration here, for how the family defines the event may depend upon its understanding of God and the world view of each family member. Again, tempered by individual beliefs, the different family members may vary in the way they view God.

Residuals from the Past

The fourth factor is related to how the family solved problems in the past and what is left over from those events. According to McCubbin and Patterson,[32] this adaptation must be considered in the outcome of a family's postcrisis adjustment as a crucial element in assessing the current crisis. It not only relates to what strategies the family used to solve the past crisis, but what issues were not completely resolved that still may be issues in this situation.

As stated earlier, the family has a need to maintain balance, and *compromise* is required to do so. However, this compromise results in a less-than-best situation where some issues will remain unresolved.[33] Those leftovers must be examined in this new situation.

A popular maxim states that success breeds success; but it is not necessarily true that failure must breed failure. A crisis may offer a family a second chance, an opportunity to correct earlier faulty problem-solving by using the past experience and desiring not to repeat the choices that led to the crisis.[34] This is true even though the old conflicts may be triggered by the current crisis and even though memory of past failure can be a burden. Crisis literature rarely mentions this, but here again is an opportunity for the exercise of *faith,* particularly the elements of forgiveness and the healing of relationships.

Readiness

The last component in the Five-Factor Model is the concept of *readiness.* This is based on a cognitive-behavioral model by Steven Brown and Linda Heath that defines pre-event coping. Their model accounts for non-random events which can be dealt with in three stages of predictability, expectedness, and preparedness.[35] I have incorporated these three stages into readiness.

The component of readiness deals with practical concerns that will prevent future crisis, and it is best explored with the family after the initial shock effects of the crisis have subsided and the equilibrium is restored. Then a counselor can help the family through the following sequence in determining readiness:

- The family must recognize that it is vulnerable to crisis in the future.
- The family must identify causative circumstances that are controllable.
- The family must choose to prepare for future events.

Because disability is a permanent condition, the family's ongoing task is to anticipate and prepare for the future, which, in itself can produce additional stress. When a child is born, a family has a developmental blueprint in mind, and knows, in general, what life stages of childhood and adolescence to expect. In contrast, nothing in life can prepare someone to be a parent of a child with a disability; these parents often feel overwhelmed by the event. The future, even tomorrow, seems uncertain.

Some parents will deny that there is a future that can, to some extent, be planned. This denial is not because of lack of education or awareness. It is, rather, the choice that is made, consciously or unconsciously, because the pain and pressures of living each day consume so much of the parents' being that becoming task oriented to future events is beyond their understanding. They have no energy to deal with any needs beyond the present. Yet it is a decisive aspect, for the more readiness that exists, the less likelihood that a transitional event will become a crisis. This will be discussed in detail in future chapters dealing with specific issues at critical transitions.

Using the AFA

A counselor can use this basic AFA framework to assess, treat, and prevent future crisis in a family. Its exploring factors will give an accurate-as-possible picture of the event and of the family, and will lead the family to develop its own skills to avert future crises.

Assessment

In counseling, assessment is a necessary first step, as well as an ongoing process. It gives the overall picture of what is occurring and can be used throughout the duration of the contact with the family. It corresponds in theory to the first stage of Egan's three-stage helping model, "Helping Clients Define and Clarify Problem Situations." [36]

The AFA utilizes a broad-band assessment approach that is not geared toward discovery of a specific pathology but focuses on several areas of the family: resources, a developmental life-stage framework, an awareness of social systems that affect the family, and an estimate of the severity of the problem. Into this assessment the counselor brings knowledge of theory, human behavior, and treatment. Egan does not mention the faith walk and the spiritual maturity of the counselor, but they are integral to the situation.

The AFA as an assessment tool is a means for the counselor to gather a great deal of information in a brief period of time. The counselor will find that the AFA lends itself to his or her particular counseling style. Each component from the Five-Factor Model is listed and broken out in detail. The counselor can then use the AFA to gather family history, to review missing resources, or to plan further interventions. The word "annotated" in the framework's title refers to the counselor's notes as each item on the list is reviewed. Completion of the AFA can be accomplished over several sessions if desired. The counselor may want to make a copy of some parts of the AFA for the counselees to take home and complete, so that they may participate in assessment and review of their current situation.

The AFA is also designed to save time by providing guidelines, so that the counselor does not have to do a lot of research if he or she is unfamiliar with specific concerns related to disabilities. The counselor also is freed from wondering if there are areas that were left unexplored, because the AFA will help provide a clear, accurate picture of the situation.

Treatment

I use the term *treatment* to describe the entire process of the help-ing relationship. Many pastoral counselors may not think of them-selves as dispensing or proscribing treatment, as it is often a medical term. But in a sense, they do.

The AFA can be used throughout this counseling treatment. It serves as a document that can concretely show the family members where gaps occur in their lives. It also can serve as a road map for goal-setting, and for learning new problem-solving and decision-making skills.

Prevention

The AFA also can help prevent future problems and crises in the family, serving as planning guide, a look at what is coming, and a predictor of what will be needed to deal with future situations. As each critical transition is presented, the appropriate AFA factors are discussed in detail. For example, the factors involved in a family's preparation for the birth of a child with a known genetic disorder are different from those accompanying a family's preparation for a young adult with Down's syndrome to leave the school system.

FOUR BASIC TYPES OF FAMILIES

Through the AFA, the counselor can also obtain an overview of the family that will allow its placement in one of four basic categories and thus determine treatment strategies. The categories are: Level 1, High Dysfunction; Level 2, Moderate Dysfunction; Level 3, Moderate Function; and Level 4, High Function. As illustrated by Figure 2–3, the line between Level 2 and Level 3 demarcates whether or not the family is functional.

There are, of course, far more than four types of families; but I have attempted to classify them this way to provide a guideline for overall counseling efforts. Using this guideline, the counselor will set priorities in assessment, treatment, and prevention according to the current level of functioning in the family. Intervention efforts will progress along a hierarchy, dependent upon the family's needs.

The counselor cannot make the assumption that because there is a child with a disability in the family there will also be dysfunction. It is well documented, however, that having a child with a disability is an added stressor for the family and presents opportunities for both dysfunction and increased functioning. The extremes between dysfunction and function are obvious, but the intervening possibilities are varying shades of gray. I have created artificial categories for the purpose of effective helping in these situations.

Although we lack a clear definition of an abnormal family, the difference between functional and dysfunctional families who have children with disabilities seems to center around one key issue, the degree of acceptance of the child with a disability, as opposed to the family's becoming frozen at an early stage in the coping process and not crossing the threshold of acceptance.[37] In families that are dysfunctional, the homeostatis of the family may depend upon keeping the child with the disability as a scapegoat, a source of problems, so as to hide and subsequently not have to deal with the real source of the conflict, the dysfunction of the parents and of the family.

Classification of Families by Function

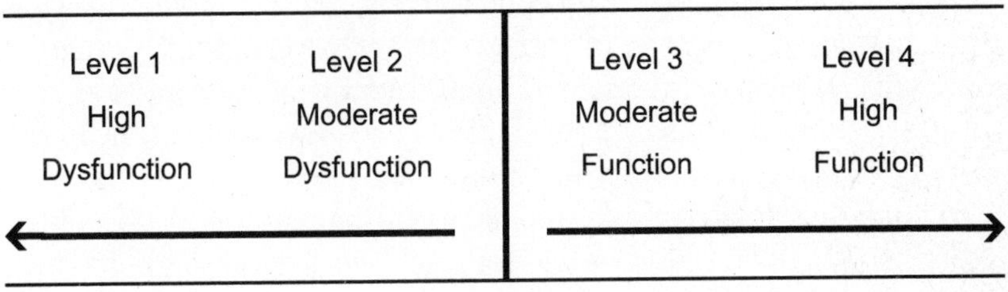

Level 1	Level 2	Level 3	Level 4
High	Moderate	Moderate	High
Dysfunction	Dysfunction	Function	Function

←——————————————————   ——————————————————→

Figure 2–3

Level 1, High Dysfunction

This is the family that would be in trouble whether or not it included a child with a disability. It has a history of high-intensity, long-duration problems which could involve substance abuse, unemployment, financial difficulties, and spouse and/or child abuse. This family is more likely to fall into a broader definition of family: a female head of household, a blended family, a family where extended members such as cousins, aunts, and uncles reside and also have caretaking roles, or a family where a grandparent is the head of household.

The child in this case is most at risk for abuse, and unfortunately, this family is least likely to receive help from a counselor, unless one person decides to break out of the system and seek assistance. This person is most likely to be the child's mother. Intensive interventions are needed to resolve basic-survival problems, as well as to meet the needs of the child with the disability. It is unlikely that the church-based counselor will be able to effectively help this family without involving other helping organizations in providing appropriate treatment, depending upon what is needed.

Level 2, Moderate Dysfunction

The Level 2 family had dysfunctional elements before the child was born; but the child with a disability was the stressor event that propelled it into crisis, and it has not recovered.

Many resulting situations are possible, but in all cases there was a shaky foundation and the birth of the child toppled the whole structure. A mother who planned to return to work after the birth may be unable to do so because of the child's needs, and the family is suffering economically because of the loss of her paycheck. One parent may view the birth of this child as punishment from God and begin or resume substance abuse. This child may require so much from the parents that the other children become neglected.

Help for this family includes rebuilding the family's foundation, either restoring the marital dyad or finding resources for the single parent.

Level 3, Moderate Functioning

Intervention for families in the third category is preventive and remediative. The counselor should examine the roles of all family members to first elicit underlying patterns of interaction. Then the counselor can present an opportunity for the family members to learn new ways of interacting to foster growth and deepen relationships. This family is at risk, and the counselor should be alert for red flags that signal the possibility of larger problematic areas.

Level 4, High Functioning

The fourth category is by far the easiest for the counselor. This family is functioning well but requires specific information. Role shifts may have begun but are not yet entrenched. The family has a spirit of cooperation and a desire to keep functioning in a healthy manner. If emotional intimacy exists in the marriage and the family members use facilitative communication skills, the counselor serves as an information source and facilitator who guides problem-solving when no therapy is necessary.

A family will not be operating in this category at all times. Generally, healthy functioning will occur between Level 3 and Level 4. Under stress, this family will drop to the third level; but if it has sufficient resources, it can regain healthy functioning. If some resources are lost or if other stressors occur, however, it can continue functioning at Level 3 and may be in danger of becoming an at-risk family.

BEHAVIORS COMMON TO DYSFUNCTIONAL FAMILIES

Behaviors of severely dysfunctional families who have children with disabilities can be grouped under eight factors.[38] Some of these factors, such as violence, neglect, and complete family isolation, are clear signals of dysfunctional families. Situations involving these factors can propel the family past the midline of functioning into dysfunction.

Other common behaviors of dysfunctional families are described below.

Loud, Chronic Complaining

Because the one receiving the direct services, the child, cannot complain, parents are placed in the role of his or her "watchdog." In this role, they may have legitimate concerns that will never be resolved to their satisfaction. There is a fine line between being perceived by a service provider as an advocate or as an obnoxious, chronic complainer. In the dysfunctional family, parents lack skills in negotiating and assertiveness, and they make continual, negative demands upon service providers.

Parents experience stress from not having their concerns heard. Further stress results if both parents are not united in their pursuit of services. If one spouse takes on the job and the other holds back, the active spouse comes to resent the other's lack of involvement.

Program Sabotage

Parents who refuse to cooperate with service providers in any manner jeopardize the welfare of their child. These parents may not see the quality or benefits of a particular program, and may not agree with the professionals' desire for certain types of placement. As the keeper of the child's records, as the one person who has the most realistic and accurate view of the child, and as the one who consistently interacts with all of the professionals who serve the child, this parent may be perceived as problematic when a disagreement occurs as to treatment or placement. Again, this will be a more serious stressor if only one parent is involved and the other takes little interest in the child's program.

Extreme Overprotectiveness

Professionals may label parents as overprotective when there is a disagreement about a particular course of treatment or placement. For example, some professionals feel that normalization is appropriate for *all* children, while parents are more likely to desire a plan that steers children toward normalization while also keeping in mind their limitations.

A family can become dysfunctional when extreme or inappropriate protectiveness hinders the child. Other overprotective behaviors that may occur in an otherwise functional family include the parents' refusal to leave the child to go out as a couple, even when a qualified baby-sitter is available; not encouraging the child to be independent, such as in self-care and dressing; or refusing to allow the child to be placed in the next higher educational level when appropriate because parents mistakenly perceive that the child is more protected in the lower setting. Or parents also might sacrifice family finances to provide the child with luxuries such as a leather coat or a CD player, or allow the child to eat any kind of food on demand, even if he or she is already overweight.

Such behavior can keep the child as a child forever. He or she is elevated to a position in the family as one whom all the others must serve, regardless of their own needs. All of this deprives the child of a normal family environment, and will cause him or her problems in other settings where all demands are not met.

Hypochondriacal Obsession

Also termed the attributional search, hypochondriacal obsession is an unrelenting search for the cause of the disability, even when all reasonable resources have been exhausted. Parents have a legitimate need to seek out causes of their child's disability to determine the best course of treatment or to determine that their other children are not at risk genetically for having children with the same problem.

However, parents may become obsessed with the "Why?" of the disability when there may never be an answer. One cause for this may be the guilt felt by the parents for having such a child, or from a need to blame themselves or others. This can lead to bitterness. When reasonable resources have been explored and parents cannot find a causative factor, it is time to give up the search.

Parents should, of course, stay abreast of medical developments as far as they are able, for the future could yield anything. But when it looks as though all reasonable efforts have been expended, it is time to stop the doctor-hopping, or this search can take on a life of its own and consume family relationships.

Open and Covert Warfare

Clear indications of violence, sexual abuse, and alcohol/drug addictions are obvious signs of open warfare in a dysfunctional family. But other factors may be harder to detect. An apparently functional family may in fact be characterized by covert warfare operations when blame, guilt, or resentment about caring for the child operates between the spouses.

These feelings may occur when parents lack communication skills that enable the family to discuss matters in a facilitative manner, or when parents are rigid authoritarians—or completely laissez faire. Or inconsistent parenting or different parenting styles may be the source of conflict between the parents. Any of these covert tactics can place a functional, Level 3 family at risk for future problems.

Symbiotic Relationships

The dysfunctional family is one that has completely isolated itself from the rest of the world, or has a delusional belief about some supernatural or special power of the child. In this case, the dysfunction is readily apparent.

However, a family's dysfunction is more subtle when one parent identifies so completely with the child with the disability that an enmeshed, symbiotic relationship is formed between that parent and the child. In response, the other parent, who may or may not have developed a normal nurturing relationship with the child, may pull away from the marital dyad. When such an imbalance occurs, the potential for problems increases, with one parent becoming further invested in the child than the other.

Avoidance

Avoidance reaches the extreme in neglect, or in denial of the disability. The gray areas of avoidance which indicate an at-risk situation occur in those families where one parent provides emotional nurturance to the child and the other distances himself or herself, moving away from family matters and into work or hobby pursuits.

To determine what may be happening in the family, the counselor could ask who keeps track of the child's educational progress, who is responsible for routine doctor and dental appointments, who arranges the child's recreational and leisure pursuits, and who teaches the child most of the skills used in the home. If one of the parents has much more responsibility for these areas than the other, this may be a sign of problems, especially if this uneven division of labor exists in combination with other problem patterns of behavior.

Psychosocial Deprivation

Some parents may be neglectful to the point of severe deprivation, ignoring the needs of the child and not making attempts to get diagnosis or treatment. This most often occurs in rural or inner-city areas when the parent has a low economic and educational level.

However, middle- and upper-class parents may become so disgruntled in dealing with formal systems that they pull out from programs, even when they are beneficial. Such parents also may ignore programs that would provide for their child's future such as SSI or Medicaid. They may not take steps for the child's placement after high school, or make provision for childcare in case of the parents' death or disability. When parents freeze at this level and stop needed interaction with resources, it is a signal that something else is occurring in the family, and the family is at risk.

The next five chapters deal with specific situations in families, particularly those periods of critical transition filled with both danger and opportunity.

CHAPTER THREE
PRENATAL AND POSTNATAL DIAGNOSES

I CLEARLY REMEMBER EXACTLY WHAT I was doing when I heard the news that President Kennedy had been shot. I was in class at Duquesne University in Pittsburgh, and in my memory I still see the black-haired woman who opened our classroom door and announced that the president had been shot. We went outdoors to listen to further news on car radios, and then proceeded into the chapel for a time of prayer. I also remember with great detail spending three days in front of the television with family and friends, eating our meals there, riveted to the TV set by the events of that tragic weekend.

Just as clearly, I can also remember the exact words of the doctor who first confirmed what I had always suspected—that my son was not behaving as a normal three-year-old should, and that he should have testing to determine his developmental level. For most parents, that memory of the moment of discovering a child's problem is frozen in time. Most parents can tell, in great detail, the story of their children's initial diagnoses. And not only are the events remembered, but the emotions felt at the time remain very vivid, too.

The emotions connected with the tragedy of President Kennedy's death have faded over time; it was an event which was very meaningful, but still external to our immediate lives. The emotions connected with a child's initial diagnosis, however, can still be recalled and felt decades later, because in essence they have never completely gone away. The news of the initial diagnosis begins the first stage of grief and sorrow, a mourning period which will become a chronic sorrow for the parents. And even though it may appear to subside, the sorrow will reappear at various times during the child's life and the family's life cycle.

The counselor may come in contact with parents who have received an initial diagnosis either before birth, at birth, or some time after the birth of a child. In addition, people with knowledge of genetic disorders in their families may come for counseling about whether to marry or to have children. The field of genetic counseling is one in which many people are turning to pastors, especially, to aid in making decisions. The main focus of this chapter is on being a helper to parents in this crisis time of the initial diagnosis, whenever it occurs.

Prenatal Diagnosis

The most crucial ethical dilemmas exist when the initial diagnosis is made before a baby is born, or when a baby born with a disability is also medically fragile. When a couple finds out they are about to become parents, they expect all to go well with the developing baby unless there is a family history of problems or unless they already have a child with a disability. Even when there is evidence that the child may be born with a disability, especially of a rare disorder, parents may be told that this is a "one-in-a-million" occurrence, and that chances still are good that this coming child will be fine.

Prenatal detection and genetics have progressed with a breathtaking rapidity in the past twenty-five years. The likelihood of detection of a disorder in a baby before birth has significantly increased over the past ten years. Parents today have prenatal options and choices that were unheard of a generation ago. It is not surprising, then, that a pastor or counselor feels inadequate to help a couple make this decision, because it is probable that he or she has no previous experience in such a situation.

The parents also may feel lost, because the news is totally unexpected and they may never have considered the possibility of having a child with a disorder, and of being faced with decisions before the child is born. Adding to the confusion is the fact that when a disorder is detected, the parents have limited time in which to make a decision for abortion or for remedial procedures. This limited time does not allow for dealing with emotions, gathering information, and making clear decisions.

Before going further, I need to explain why I am mentioning abortion in a Christian counseling book. My personal stance is against abortion; to me, the baby is a life that is already known to God and I cannot take control of whether or not that life continues. However, some parents who learn of problems in their unborn children are offered this option by doctors. The parents may come to the counselor or pastor to obtain assistance and guidance in making their decision. That counselor or pastor then faces the delicate task of being a guide and a helper on this crucial issue, while making sure that, no matter what his or her own position is on abortion, the couple is ultimately responsible for the decision.

Prenatal Testing Procedures

Problems in unborn children can be detected in many ways. The following brief review of procedures is by no means intended to be medically complete; but it will provide the counselor with a working knowledge of the terminology involved.

Fetal Ultrasound. The fetal ultrasound is probably the most widely known diagnostic procedure. Its use has increased substantially for normal pregnancies, whereas an ultrasound was given only for suspected problems about ten years ago. The ultrasound, considered to be a safe procedure, uses sound waves that bounce off the baby and show the outline of its organs and limbs. It is used to check the size and position of the baby, pinpointing the delivery date more accurately. In addition, the sex of the baby can be determined, as well as the number of babies in the womb. The ultrasound can also detect spina bifada, hydrocephalus, certain skeletal disorders, congenital heart disease, and other disorders.[1]

Because the ultrasound predicts a more precise birth date than in the past, there have been fewer induced deliveries. In addition, women who see a "picture" of their baby are more likely to bond to the unborn child and take measures to promote its health. In one study, women who saw the sonogram were more likely to quit smoking, which resulted in higher birth-weight babies.[2]

Amniocentesis. An amniocentesis is performed by inserting a needle through the mother's abdomen into the uterus and taking a sample of the amniotic fluid. It is best performed at the sixteenth or seventeenth week of pregnancy. Analysis of the fluid will reveal the gender of the child as well as detect disorders. It is most often used to detect Down syndrome and spina bifada through measuring blood alpha-fetoprotein. The chance of miscarriage from this procedure is between one in two hundred to one in three hundred.[3]

Chorionic Villus Sampling(CVS). CVS removes a tiny amount of tissue from the placenta to examine the chorionic villi, which look like tiny hairs. It is performed at the eighth or ninth week of pregnancy, when the sac holding the fetus is six-tenths of an inch in diameter. The results from a chromosome analysis of a CVS can be given within a few hours.[4] There is a concern about miscarriage from CVS because the rate is estimated to be from 4 in 100 to 1 in 130.

Blood Testing of Pregnant Mother. New tests that use a sample of the mother's blood are being developed and may eventually appear for public use. Blood tests are currently being used in controlled studies as a screening before amniocentesis, not as a substitute for the procedure.[5] In addition, other researchers are in the beginning stages of testing maternal blood samples for several genetic disorders, but it is not known when and if these will be available for general use.[6]

DNA Analysis. A blood sample can be drawn from either parent before a child is conceived to detect disorders such as sickle cell anemia or thalassemia. Screenings are often held for populations likely to develop these disorders, which are related to people whose heritage is in certain geographic locations. When adults are screened and results show that they have the disorder or are carriers, they face decisions about marriage and children.

Fetal Surgery. One of the newer and certainly more amazing procedures is fetal surgery, where prebirth repair can be performed on the baby, who then remains in the womb until its birth. Some examples of this are the repair of a baby's diaphragmatic hernia, and of another baby's bladder which was blocked and filled with urine. Both corrective procedures were performed successfully.[7]

Fetal reduction. This procedure requires a more heart-wrenching decision for parents. When an ultrasound shows two or more babies developing in the womb and there is a problem with one or more, parents have a choice of procedures. In a recent case, when the mother was carrying twins and one baby showed a problem that threatened the life of the other, the parents were offered three alternatives. They could continue the pregnancy and hope that the "good" baby did well despite the problems caused by the "bad" twin. They could choose an abortion of both. Or they could choose ". . . selective termination, where air is injected into the heart of the 'bad' twin, and it dies."[8] They opted for the latter procedure.

In another case, the mother had undergone in vitro fertilization and had a half-hour to decide how many of eight embryos to have implanted. She and her husband chose to have six implanted, and amazingly, all but one "took." The mother was a small woman of only 105 pounds, and chose to carry only two babies to term, as her chance of having five live babies was slim. She said that it was hard to choose, in essence, to destroy three of her five children, but faced with this situation, the couple agreed to a fetal reduction of three.[9]

Our technology is far ahead of our ability to form absolute ethical, moral, and spiritual positions on these crucial situations. So it may seem like an overwhelming task to form a base of knowledge and ethics from which to counsel parents in these situations. The counselor needs to be certain of his or her own personal stance on the issue (hopefully based on a sound biblical perspective) and yet be facilitative enough to help parents who must bear the ultimate responsibility for these decisions.[10]

POSTNATAL TESTING

All states have mandatory blood testing of infants for certain metabolic disorders (such as phenylketonuria, PKU) that are remediable through medication and/or diet.

Other tests can help diagnose a variety of disorders or disabilities in children after birth. For example, a test which measures excess sodium and chlorine in the child's sweat is used to detect cystic fibrosis. A chromosome analysis of the child's blood sample with a resulting karyotype is used to detect genetic disorders.[11] (A karyotype is made from a photograph of chromosomes that is taken after drawn blood is grown in a culture. The photograph shows the chromosomes as they appear naturally; each chromosome image is cut out and arranged in pairs. From that arrangement, the geneticist can identify abnormalities.)

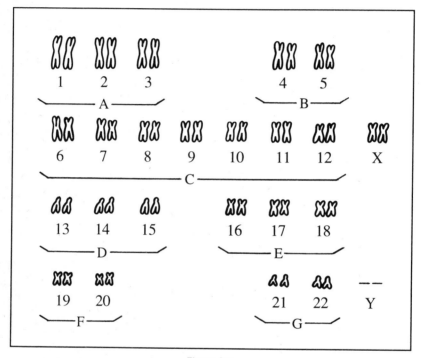

Figure 3-1
Normal Female Karyotype
The display shows 46 chromosomes, 22 nonsex pairs and two X chromosomes.
Courtesy of Eastern Virginia Medical School, Cytogenetics Division,
Department of Pediatrics.

Many genetic disorders are not yet identifiable by karyotype. In those cases, the child's symptoms are compared with the symptoms of over three hundred identifiable genetic disorders, and the doctor makes a diagnosis on the basis of the best match.

GENETIC DISORDERS

A relatively small percentage of disabilities is attributable to genetic disorders, but a discussion of them is included here because the disability that results is permanent and often of the more severe type. Researchers have now located seventeen hundred genes on human chromosomes, seven hundred within the past few years. Fifty-three of these seven hundred are causes of inherited disorders, such as retardation, childhood tumors, and growth disorders.[12]

A Human Genome Project is in progress to develop screening for thousands of rare genetic diseases. (A genome is a set of chromosomes with the genes they contain.) This is the largest genetic project to date and the possibilities for future children are enormous.

We all carry a number of defective genes because genetic variety is necessary for survival of the human race. Some defective genes even carry hidden benefits, such as protection against diseases in certain parts of the world. But while genetic research is expanding medical capabilities, we must be careful that being able to pinpoint genetic disorders does not lead to selective breeding or worse, holding parents accountable for not aborting a child with a known genetic disorder.[13]

Keeping in mind that a defect does not necessarily result in a disability, the causes of developmental defects in humans are generally as follows:

—known genetic transmission, 20 percent
—chromosomal aberration, 3–5 percent
—environmental causes (radiation, infections, maternal metabolic imbalance, drugs, and environmental chemicals), 6–10 percent
—unknown causes, 65–75 percent.[14]

Basics of Genetics

Although a detailed discussion of genetic disorders is beyond the range of this book, some basic discussion is necessary to promote understanding of the disabilities of children.[15]

Normal human cells each have forty-six chromosomes, except the sperm and egg cells, which each have twenty-three. Problems are caused by extra chromosomes, not enough chromosomes, or improper location of chromosomes. Chromosomal problems are not curable, although medical, educational, and therapeutic interventions can increase the quality of life for children with genetic disorders. Some chromosomal abnormalities are apparent from a karyotype, but relatively few disorders have become specifically located. See Figure 3–2 for common terms related to karyotyping that a counselor may encounter.

Chromosomal Abnormalities

Trisomy	—	existence of an extra chromosome
Monosomy	—	having one less chromosome than is normal
Deletion	—	a piece of the chromosome is missing
Translocation	—	two chromosomes are attached to each other
Mosaicism	—	some cells are normal, but other cells have abnormal chromosomes

Figure 3–2

Classification of Genetic Disorders

Genetic disorders are classified by how they are inherited:

Autosomal dominant. If one parent has the disorder, 50 percent of the children will have the disease (an example is Huntington's disease).

Autosomal recessive. If both parents are carriers of the recessive gene, and the child received both recessive genes, the child will have the disorder (an example is PKU, an enzyme deficiency that can cause mental retardation unless a special diet is employed).

These types of disorders are the basis for our laws that prohibit close relatives from marrying.

X-linked recessive. These genes are carried by a mother on one of her two X chromosomes (examples are hemophilia, color blindness, and muscular dystrophy).

Multifactorial. The genes and environment combine in an unknown manner (examples are cleft lip, cleft palate, and spina bifada).

Down's syndrome. One of the most common and identifiable genetic disorders, Down's syndrome, can result from three causes:

—94 percent of cases are from Trisomy 21.
—2.4 percent are from mosaicism.
—3.6 percent are from translocation.[16]

Down's syndrome is not always caused by maternal age: 70 percent is from nondisjunction (improper forming) of the egg; 20 percent is from nondisjunction of the sperm, and 10 percent is from translocation.[17] This classification of causality presents a slightly different percentage for translocation. The two sets of statistics are not contradictory, but indicative of the ranges found by different researchers.

IMPLICATIONS FOR COUNSELING

Attitudes Toward Testing

Several positions exist regarding prenatal or preconception procedures for detection of disorders. To some, the procedure is done to prevent the birth of a child with a disorder. For example, if a couple is screened for Tay-Sachs disease, which is always eventually fatal to a child, they can make a decision not to risk having children at all. They can also decide that if there is a pregnancy, they will have a test and then have an abortion if the child has the disorder.

A more positive approach is to use test results as information to help the couple prepare for the birth of the child, gather information, build support, and to grow in faith. Some women will choose not to have any testing at all, deciding that they will keep the child no matter what. Some doctors will not allow certain mothers considered to be high risk (such as those over age thirty-five) to waive the tests unless they sign formal documents releasing the doctor from responsibility for any problems. This is the result of the current litigious climate in the United States, where parents sue doctors for the births of infants with problems, often basing the suit on the doctors' responsibility to detect the disorders prenatally.

Helping Couples Make Decisions

The counselor who meets with a couple expecting a child with a disorder is dealing with a crisis situation. If the procedure used was amniocentesis, it was performed at around the sixteenth week of pregnancy, and the results probably came in about two weeks. The parents must then decide immediately if they are going to continue the pregnancy.

There are genetic counselors at genetic testing centers; but they deal in facts, not values. They present all sides of the situation and the parents are left alone to make the decision. There are pastoral counselors who specialize in genetic counseling; but not all couples will have access to them, particularly if the families do not reside in a large city. Thus they may turn to their local pastor or Christian counselor for help in making this decision.

The counselor cannot, at this point, give directive advice, telling the couple what they should or should not do. Besides being open to a possible lawsuit at some point in the future, the counselor may also eventually be blamed by the couple for their negative feelings, no matter what the decision is. A better stance is to choose a course that will include a problem-solving approach, and include liberal doses of Christian hope.

In this crisis situation, the counselor will have to get a perspective of where the couple is in their faith walk. In all probability, they are at a crisis point not only in their lives, but also in their faith. They are being called to a deeper walk for which they are not prepared, which they did not expect, and which no one could predict. They are in anguish, and they may be searching for blame: Was it a sin one of them committed? Was it something the mother ate or drank or did? They are feeling like victims at this point, and they are also in mourning. Suddenly, the healthy child they were expecting is gone, and another is expected in its place. Their parental dreams and hopes have been shattered.

This is a time for a gentle ministry. The parents are asking "Why?" and then, "Can we cope? How can we cope?" They need to experience God's love for them, as well as the counselor's love for them, and his or her willingness to share in their sorrow. They must be allowed to be angry at themselves and at God, and they also must be allowed to state their fear and helpless feelings. This is a matter in which prayer is central. I would encourage a time of prayer and Scripture reading as an integral part of counseling these parents. Psalm 139 and Romans 8:28 provide a valuable perspective here.

Without counseling, the parents' sorrow could dominate them until it becomes despair. The counselor can employ positive methods that will give them another view of life. It would be extremely helpful for this couple to talk to another parent who had a child with a disability, or to even meet a child or an adult with a disability, such as Down syndrome. Ideally, a Christian parent who has been coping successfully would be a tremendous resource. Some organizations have established parent-to-parent groups that could be of help. These groups have various names such as Pilot Parents or Parents Helping Parents, and there are chapters all over the United States.

In the counseling session, the counselor will have to let go of whatever decision the parents are making. It is the parents' responsibility, after all. This is a time to discuss a positive, biblical perspective of God's mercy, love, provision, and strength. You may be able to offer the support of church members through this time of preparation and after the birth, so that they will not feel alone.

The couple may decide to abort the baby—and later regret that decision. The counselor's position can only be one of acceptance of the person and of servanthood in helping the person (the mother, the father, or both) work through forgiveness, both of self and from God. I realize as I am writing this that there are some Christians who take a more liberal position on abortion than I am presenting here. I cannot take that position because it is not part of my theology. I would like to convey the concept that although doctors making the diagnosis may tell people, "It's bad news," a child with a disability is not necessarily "bad," and the decision to abort should not be automatic.

A Baby Born with a Disability

When a baby is born we usually expect all to go well and see the mother and child home in a few days. Sometimes, unfortunately, things do not go well and expectations are not realized. Any of the following can occur:

- A child is stillborn.
- Complications develop that leave both mother and child temporarily seriously ill but without permanent effects.
- A child is born with a problem that calls for a prolonged hospital stay, but it is resolved without permanent effect.
- A child is born with a disability and a life-threatening situation.
- A child is born with a life-threatening condition but does not have a diagnosed disability.
- A child is born with a disability that is not life-threatening.

The last three conditions are the focus of this section. A child born with a disability and a life-threatening condition has been the subject of legal and ethical battles recently, resulting in the "Baby Doe" ruling that prohibits withholding treatment from a child because of the disability. These battles, generating wide-ranging discussions on the issue of quality of life, are taking place on a number of fronts and have yet to be completely resolved.

The Child with a Life-Threatening Problem

Parents who have a child born with a life-threatening problem may be asked to make a decision regarding treatment of their child at a

45

time when they are in crisis. A discussion of the multitude of conditions that can cause these problems is not relevant here. What is of interest to the counselor is the emotional state of the parents and the role of the counselor or pastor who is called in to help.

A very sick baby will most likely be placed in a Neonatal Intensive Care Unit (NICU), or Pediatric Intensive Care Unit (PICU), which in itself is a frightening place. The baby looks so small and fragile, and is hooked up to more wires and tubes than one would ever think could possibly be connected to such a tiny body. The NICU is full of machines, people are bustling about, and a sense of urgency surrounds the babies.

In this setting, what should have been a time of joy and elation for the parents is turned into fear, doubt, and confusion. Parents are asked to digest vast amounts of information without full comprehension, unless one of them is in the medical profession. They are then asked to make decisions regarding extraordinary measures, difficult operations, and often astronomical costs. These decisions often have to be made quickly, without time to fully comprehend the overall situation. Often, the baby will be transported to another hospital in the same city, or even to another city for care and subsequent treatment. The mother is still recuperating from the birth and cannot travel right away to be with the baby. The travel distance also may be a problem for the parents who want to be with the baby, but are unable to afford it or need to care for their other children.

During this crisis, the counselor can provide emotional support to the parents, help them sort out their feelings, facilitate understanding of the medical situation as much as possible, and help them through the decision-making process. In addition, parents may need practical help with transportation, lodging, care for other children, and meals. Church ministries can help provide those needs. The counselor should also contact the hospital social worker and the hospital chaplain for whatever assistance they could provide.

The Child Born with a Disability

When a child is born with a disability but is not medically fragile, the parents are in an initial state of shock, much as the parents who find out that the baby they are still expecting has a problem. The hospital stay for the mother and child may not be extensive and help by the counselor in the hospital setting will vary according to the parents' needs at the time.

The ability of medical personnel to convey such news in a compassionate manner also varies. If the news has been conveyed to the parents in a matter-of-fact or offhand way, they experience additional negative feelings. Not only are they dealing with grief over the child's condition, but they are feeling their own inadequacy as parents to produce a normal child. Being treated without understanding by their doctors contributes to the parents' despair.

In all fairness to doctors, however, I do not want to be condemning. Some doctors are marvelously compassionate, empathic, and of real help to parents. Others are not, and I often wonder if these professionals are so touched by sorrow themselves that they must remain objective and rational in order to keep their own feelings under control. I do not believe any doctor would deliberately be unkind to parents in this situation.

THE NEWBORN AT HOME

When the child is at home, the reality of the situation may leave the parents feeling overwhelmed. They are coming to realize this is the beginning of a long-term challenge, and of joys and frustrations that will persist over several years.

Their fears may become intensified at this point as the specialized care given by professionals in the hospital now must be given by the parents. Most new parents, especially first-time ones, have some doubts and fears about their inability to care properly for the newborn. I can remember being greatly relieved that my mother was present to help me give my first child his first bath. I didn't know where to begin!

The Medically Involved Newborn

Parental feelings of inadequacy intensify even more when the child has a disability, and especially when there is a medical problem; they may be afraid of doing something wrong as they administer medication or give other assistance. In addition, the child may need to be fed more often, or he or she may take a long time to nurse, and the parents may find it difficult to rest.

The father may worry about returning to work and leaving the mother alone. Each noise and grunt the baby makes may become a cause for alarm. The parents may need to have one or more of their own parents come into the home to help. Meanwhile, they may find themselves dealing with medical bills and trying to sort out insurance claims. If extensive treatment is required, they may even have to look into becoming eligible for Medicaid.

Effects of the Newborn on Other Children

Other children in the household are affected by the newborn. Older children may be required to assume additional duties as the parents shift their energies toward the baby. Younger ones may not get the attention to which they are accustomed, and may not fully understand why this baby requires so much of their parents' time and concern. They may not be able to hold and play with the baby as they had expected.

Infant Stimulation Programs

The pediatrician may recommend an infant stimulation program, but the idea of taking a new baby out to classes may seem strange to the parents. Also, most programs include home visits of some type and include some physical therapy exercises for parents to do at home with the baby. This may all seem overwhelming to parents who didn't expect to begin all of this outside contact so soon, let alone have strangers coming to their home and, in a sense, invading their family privacy.

Despite these possibilities, the counselor should encourage infant stimulation and contact with other parents who have children with disabilities. Although these may be seen to be a burden at first, the long-term results are well worth the effort. It is a tremendous relief to find out that you are not the only parent who has a child with a problem, that there are others who are coping, and that there is a real resource in the sharing of information with these parents. The baby also makes developmental gains by being in the program.

PROBLEMS FACING PARENTS OF NEWBORNS WITH DISABILITIES

Dealing with Professionals

Parents of a baby with a disability have many professionals in their lives, many more than parents of children who may only see a pediatrician for routine care. An "extended family" that may include a social worker, psychologist, neurologist, physical therapist, teacher, case manager, speech therapist, or surgeon is acquired by all children once a diagnosis of a disability is made, whether as an infant or later.

Parents, themselves, may become medical "experts" and may, at times, disagree with doctors' decisions regarding treatment. Many parents have a knowledge of the child's specific disorder that is equal to the doctor's, because they have made a determined quest to seek out knowledge regarding their child's disability. They may even have information that the doctor does not.

Dealing with Others

As the family members decide how they are going to explain the child's condition to others, they find that their child quickly acquires a label. Particular labels are more acceptable to the parents than others, some being more socially acceptable, and some requiring a lot of explanation. A child may only have a diagnosis of "developmentally delayed," which is vague and unclear. The diagnosis may be mental retardation, which still carries a stigma of sorts. Down syndrome is easy to explain to people, because it is well known. A genetic disorder, such as Werdnig-Hoffman disease, an autosomal recessive disorder of unknown origin, requires much explanation. I have often felt as though I should carry index cards printed with an explanation of my son's disorder to hand out to people who do not know him, because the explaining gets tiresome.

Parents will face many new stressors, in addition to deciding how to tell others. Additional stressors include not knowing specifically what is wrong with the child; dealing with reactions from people in public when the parents go out with the baby, who may appear abnormal; finding competent baby-sitters; and trying to function as a normal family.

Church Attendance

Church attendance can put a strain on the family members, so they may not attend church with the baby because it is too great an effort. This is more likely when the church nursery is not able to provide proper care for the baby. Parents of the child with a disability may find that they no longer have the time or energy to participate in ministry or fellowship groups—probably at a time when they need friends and support the most.

Using the Annotated Family Appraisal

The AFA is intended as a broad-based instrument to be used with families at all stages of the life span. The following discussion deals with specific elements at this newborn-child stage. The details presented here are to supplement the AFA as it is presented in Appendix I.

The Event

In a sense, the source of the event is external, because the birth of a child with a disability is one in which the family has had no control. There are elements of dismemberment, because of the loss of the normal child that was expected, and also of accession, because of the arrival of the child with an unexpected disability. Demoralization may be present if the family members feel disgrace and shame, depending upon the reaction of significant others in their lives. Demoralization may also be present if the child's condition is attributed to an action of the parents, such as alcohol or drug use, or exposure to chemicals in a job.

A status shift in the family may occur both in income and in roles. A mother who expected to return to work now may be unable to do so, and the loss of her income may bring significant financial restraints upon the family. The effects of income and roles may overlap. It is important to look at how much this will change the family's life and at the extent of the short- and long-term effects. The family needs to be aware of these matters so as to be in as much control of the situation as possible.

There may be unrealistic expectations of each parent at this time about how the other should handle the challenge and its resulting grief, sorrow, and shock. One parent (usually the father) may immerse himself in work and leave all of the concerns of the baby to the mother. Conflicts may result over household chores, care for the baby, or care for other children.

Resources

In addition to the resources listed on the AFA, specific concerns are related to the newborn or newly diagnosed child. Possible areas for exploration are:

Will insurance cover medical costs, tests, specialized equipment, and evaluations, both psychological and physical?

Does the family have the ability to pay for capable baby-sitters?

What is available in the community to help the family?

Does the family need help to continue with church attendance?

Who is the primary caregiver and what will change in his or her life?

Can the parents still find time for prayer and Bible study as a family, as a couple, and as individuals?

What does the family have available to help it maintain a life that is as normal and balanced as possible?

Family Definition of the Event

The family definition of this event will be fluid and will change from time to time as the family members attempt to make sense of what has happened and how they will deal with it. The first reaction of the parents is shock. Then reality filters in in small, manageable doses. Parents need to keep their self-esteem intact throughout all of this process, yet so often they are angry at the feeling of being at the mercy of others in their lives and the life of the child.[18]

Parental reactions may differ with the nature of the child's disability, sometimes even with the gender of the child. For some reason, fathers are more able to be accepting of a disorder in a daughter than in a son. Research has not shown that the key to predicting reactions in parents is by the nature of the disability. Rather, the parents' individual personalities seem to be more of a factor.[19] I suspect, however, that parental reactions to a physical disability in a child with normal intelligence are different than when mental retardation is the disability; and both of these are different than when there is multi-involved disability, such as cerebral palsy. The differences involve having different sets of problems and circumstances to work through, combined with all of the factors in this model.

The counselor needs to give the family the "gift of time" in defining the event.[20] Parents and siblings will travel through many events connected with this child that may change their definition considerably as the reality of the situation becomes more apparent. The challenge for the counselor is to allow time for the initial grieving and yet move the parents forward, ever so gently, so that they do not become stuck in that first stage of grief and never move on to where their coping mechanisms can begin operating.

While we know grief is present, the literature does not present a clear understanding of the parents' grief process when a child has a disability.[21] Many counselors try to define whether the grief is of a relatively short term or is ongoing. More than thirty years ago, Simon Olshansky first defined the concept of chronic sorrow when there is a child with

51

a disability.[22] This view is that the feelings of grief are re-evoked periodically over the life of the child. Those times that are most likely to reawaken grief are the significant, critical transitions of the child and family. They are discussed throughout this book.

The best explanation of grief is probably that it is twofold: The first mourning occurs for the normal, desired child that will never be, coupled with sorrow in seeing the suffering or lack of ability of the present child; the second mourning is the ongoing, chronic sorrow that will reoccur at times all through life.

The counselor also must be aware that this is a lifelong journey for these parents, and progress of the child and of the emotional life of the family may seem to be on a roller coaster. In reality, a family can become increasingly stronger in coping and in faith by meeting challenge after challenge, and in facing the fact that life will always hold some sort of challenge for this child.

On an episode of the TV series "Life Goes On," Corky, the adolescent with Down syndrome, was in trouble with the coach for making an inappropriate comment. Corky's mother asked her husband, "How long will we have to go on speaking to others for him, explaining for him?" That statement contains a great deal of frustration and yet an admission of reality.

Residual Past

The family's leftovers from past crises will vary according to the age of the parents. In general, young parents will have less experience with crises as a couple, while older parents will naturally have more. The counselor must gather the family history to determine whether counseling that deals with past unresolved matters would be beneficial. If a couple already is experiencing problems, this new event may propel the family into crisis.

Readiness

The question of "Why?" is usually one of the first asked by parents after they learn the "What." In their desire to find out the "Why?" parents may engage in an unproductive attributional search that continues over many years. There are some valid reasons for looking for causes of disability, such as determining genetic causality, or trying to determine as exact a diagnosis as possible in hopes of obtaining treatment. But if the object of the search is to affix blame, when no apparent fault is present, the search becomes destructive. When parents become stuck on finding a cause after all reasonable efforts have been exhausted, they block themselves and their children from moving on in life.

This futile search for a cause also prevents the family from looking forward and making future plans. When such a search becomes the all-consuming, central focus, attention shifts away from what the child needs to become as productive a person as possible. The "Why?" stage may last quite a while for some, and not as long for others. My own "Why?" kept resurfacing for years, until one day I discovered there was no answer to the question that made any sense, and therefore there was no value in continuing that search. Then I experienced a freedom from releasing that issue to God, and adding it to my list of questions to ask him when I get to heaven, such as, "Why mosquitoes?"

Although this was an unpredictable event, it is the task of the counselor to help parents sort through elements so they feel less helpless and more in control. If the child is so medically fragile that the outcome is uncertain, little can be done except to become aware of the possibilities and discuss tentative courses of action. When Charlene was in danger of death after two years of fighting the ravages of leukemia, her mother, Helen, planned funeral arrangements. However, Helen continued to confer with the doctors as to the best possible treatment procedures and continued to believe in the possibility of God's intervening hand to produce a miracle. I believe that it was that balance of preparedness and faith that kept Helen intact throughout Charlene's two months on a respirator and her subsequent death.

If the child has a developmental disability with a somewhat predictable course, then the parents can begin to look at possible courses of action to enhance that child's life. They need to see that they are not helpless, that they can prepare and plan by projecting their child's future needs and examining how they can manage their own lives. Some days this task will seem impossible, but with a healthy perspective it can be done.

PRACTICAL HELPS FOR PARENTS

The following list of practical helps for parents can apply at this newborn/infant stage, as well as at many other times in the child's later life.

It is crucial that parents obtain all the information they need in plain language from all professionals involved. When professionals use jargon and highly technical terms parents should not hesitate to ask for a "translation" of anything they do not understand.

It is extremely helpful to keep a notebook about the child that describes every interaction with someone regarding him or her, whether it is in person or by phone. This may seem tedious, but it will be extremely valuable in helping the parent remember what was said, and as a reference for the future. We only remember 50 percent of what we hear; memory quickly fades over time.

In this notebook, write the date, the name of the professional, and all pertinent information, especially medication instructions or procedures. In addition, write down questions and concerns whenever they occur. Then, when visiting a doctor or another professional about the child, the parent can take the notebook, have the question at hand, and jot down the answer. Mothers should not be automatically assigned the job of maintaining the notebook; the father, or another family member, can also write in questions and concerns.

Parents should also keep a separate notebook, or a section of the first notebook, that records developmental events. Over the years, parents will have to tell professionals repeatedly all of the child's "firsts," such as when the child first lifted his or her head, or first ate solid food. Records of weight and height, and the schedule of all inoculations should also be kept. Although much of this information is also kept in medical records, it is not unusual for medical records to be lost. So, especially for children with developmental disabilities, it is helpful for parents to have their own records, even if the official records are never lost.

Parents also need to care for themselves, and get proper rest and nutrition. Other family members or a church fellowship can offer assistance to prevent parental exhaustion, realizing the parents may be reluctant to ask for help. Providing sitters for the other children, meals, or transportation can be very helpful to these struggling families. If you are the pastor, you can rally church members to help. If you are a counselor, you can, with their permission, contact the parents' pastor to suggest such assistance and also provide a list of concrete, specific needs.

As I stated earlier, parents need to know they are not alone, and the counselor can reinforce this by helping them find appropriate organizations that will help them, if only so they can hear someone say "I've been there." Most cities have several organizations and agencies to help parents; if you are in a rural area, contact the national organization that is applicable. Information on organizations and publications can be found in Appendix II.

Parents must realize their baby with a developmental disability will be late in achieving the tasks of growth and development—but that such changes *will* occur. Counselors should encourage parents to proceed as though their child were normal in creating a positive environment to foster this development. They should put up a bright mobile, make tactile objects available to the baby, and stimulate play and encourage language by playing peek-a-boo, reading aloud, and singing. A nonbreakable mirror is also fun for baby. This environment will help the child continue to progress at his or her own rate.

Robert Schuller has said, "Anyone can count the seeds in an apple, but only God can count the apples in a seed."[23] So it is with a child with a disability. Anyone can read a test result or *IQ* score, but *no one* can predict the limits on an individual child. Many times, I have seen children progress beyond doctors' dire predictions. No one can predict the influence of a loving, nurturing environment, or of a teacher who believes in the potential of the child. No one can predict God's workings in the individual.

Counselors can encourage parents who do not see much response in a new baby, keeping in mind that the daily progress in the child is not as important as parental progress in accepting, loving, and nurturing the child. Also, by remaining steadfast in their faith, parents will have a resource of strength and hope. As they realize that their child is wonderfully and fearfully made, known to God before he or she was born, they will be able to rejoice in his or her seemingly small steps of progress.

Counselors should stress how important it is for the mother to hold and cuddle her baby so mother-baby bonding occurs. Some research has shown that parental bonding is less likely to occur with unresponsive babies, because the mother has a more difficult time becoming emotionally attached to an infant who does not seem to respond, and therefore acts in a less nurturing manner; this sets up the cycle of not bonding.[24] Perhaps because of this, babies with disabilities are at high risk for child abuse and death, a possibility demonstrated in New York City, where the number of babies with disabilities who died from abuse was of a much higher proportion than normal infants.[25]

Parents need permission to express their feelings of anger, confusion, of being overwhelmed, or of being frightened, so they will not take out those feelings on the child, either by direct abuse or by neglect. Parents also need to maintain the marital relationship, so the child does not become the focus of the marriage. If the infant is in the hospital, the parents need to give themselves a break from twenty-four-hour vigils. They should take an hour for dinner together and try to spend some nights sleeping at home or in a hospice if that is available. No matter what happens to the child, the marital relationship will remain, and it needs nurturing.

Other children also need attention, so it is important that the parents make a commitment to maintain as normal a family life as possible, even though this can only be in small doses. A first family outing after the birth might be as simple as a picnic. Church members could show some special attention and care to the other children by taking them for an outing once a week if the parents are required to spend a lot of their time caring for the child with the disability.

These are trying times for a family as it deals with the initial diagnosis and tries to restore its balance. The counselor must be sensitive to the many unique issues of each of these families, patiently traveling step by step with them on these journeys with their many setbacks, detours, and challenges. The following chapters will look at the family at other stages of the child's life, outlining both counselor strategies and practical helps.

CHAPTER FOUR

THE TODDLER/PRESCHOOL YEARS

THE TODDLER/PRESCHOOL YEARS are times of rapid growth and development for children. A vast difference exists between a two-year-old and a five-year-old child. As they watch other children progress through these years, parents of a child with a disability are increasingly aware of what is not occurring in their child according to a normal developmental schedule.

Depending upon what has occurred with their child, parents can be in one of the following four different stages:

- The child was diagnosed as having a problem when an infant, and now is in some type of program.
- The child is first diagnosed as having a problem during these years.

- The child was developing normally, but had an accident or illness that resulted in a developmental disability.
- The parents have a vague suspicion that things are not quite right with the child, but a diagnosis is not made.

The counselor must understand the specific situation of each family in order to be effective. We cannot make an assumption about what is happening in the family based only on the age of the child. As we look at the specific circumstances of each of these stages, we can broaden our base of understanding and then develop strategies that are appropriate for helping the family.

DIAGNOSIS IN THE FIRST YEAR

When a child is diagnosed as disabled within the first year, the parents are already "broken in" to the world of disabilities by the time the child reaches the toddler years. I use that term because it is as though one enters a whole different world than parents of children who are developing without problems. One difference is that these parents have been taking their children on a regular basis to many doctors, therapists, and psychologists, far more than other parents. The parents may also have been involved with infant stimulation services from as early as when the child was six weeks old.

The counselor can help families in this stage in several ways. The first way is to encourage them to reach out to other parents for support for themselves, and eventually to be a support to other parents, such as is found in a parent-to-parent support group. The "experienced" parents may be familiar with community services that could meet the needs of the "new" parents' child. Also, a parent of a toddler who is new to the group may be able to help parents of newborns with disabilities. Being active in a group will enable parents to keep up with information that would benefit their child, and would also prevent their feeling isolated.

A second way the counselor can help is to encourage the parents as the child grows out of infancy, which forces the parents to face the realities of developmental lags. As they watch other children of the same ages walk, talk, feed themselves, and complete toilet training, the differences in their own children become more marked than when they were infants. They may hear other parents discussing various preschools, home playgroups, and other activities and feel left out.

Using the church nursery or other baby-sitting arrangements may become more difficult as the child requires more than just having a bottle, diaper change, and a nap, and becomes larger and harder to carry. Getting the child in and out of the car, even changing the diaper, if that is necessary, become more difficult during this period.

The parents may realize at this point that they are going to be connected to community services, and perhaps medical services, virtually forever. Ironically, research has shown that parents with greater involvement in "the system" experience higher degrees of stress than parents who do not get involved.[1] This puts these parents into a double bind. They need the help, and yet by accepting it, they must allow strangers to become involved in details of the family's life. The strangers are necessary and well-meaning; but privacy is sacrificed and family boundaries are expanded far beyond those of other families.

The counselor should be sensitive to this dynamic and not automatically label parents as resistant if they seem reluctant to make these changes in their lives. The counselor can help parents by teaching them assertiveness skills that will enable them to deal with outside helpers. One need for these skills is evident when parents feel intimidated by professionals and, as a result, become angry. They then become aggressive or pull back, and neither strategy helps them obtain the help their child needs. Assertiveness training can help parents retain the sense of control they may have lost when their child was born.

Parents may also need instruction in time management so they can carve out some time for themselves, both as individuals and as a couple. This is important to the family, as well as to the couple; so the counselor should stress that the parents should feel no guilt about creating time for themselves. Without this understanding, the father may feel guilty about devoting any time at all to a hobby or leisure pursuits, because his job keeps him out of the home so much already. The mother, if she has been at home as the primary caregiver for the first few years, may be longing to rejoin the mainstream of life, especially if the child is in no medical danger. She may be seeking some outlet for recreation and leisure, or perhaps an outside job or a return to school. The couple may desire a vacation or a weekend alone. Once parents accept their need for time to themselves, however, finding care for the child may be so difficult that it seems easier to once again give up on the idea.

Sometimes parents in this circumstance may be locked into a pattern of behavior which includes living up to a false image of what they think others expect of them. They may feel trapped and unable to break out of the routine. The counselor can help parents understand these traps—and then avoid them.

THE CHILD DIAGNOSED DURING TODDLER YEARS

When diagnosis occurs during the toddler years, the parents may have been experiencing some problems in caring for the child. They may have been comparing their child with other toddlers, and asking themselves a lot of questions regarding their own child's behavior. Because there was no explanation for the problems before the diagnosis, a great amount of speculation and frustration has occurred. And the parents' fears and concerns may have been rebuffed by doctors.

A diagnosis usually follows several examinations. Parents may need assistance in understanding the terminology of all the resulting reports, which may be physical, psychological, and neurological. Also, parents may have trouble coming to grips with a doctor's negative prognosis which seems to shred any remnants of hope.

In addition to empathic listening, the counselor can validate the parents' feelings of disappointment or despair, while helping them focus on the positive aspects of the child. This focus should occur in an atmosphere of seeing God's hand not only on the child, but also in their lives. The counselor's willingness to share both their despair and their joy at inches of progress will be a powerful expression of God's love, for them and for their child.

Diagnosis of a child at a young age can be difficult when the cause of the developmental disability is unknown. Unless specific medical problems or an easily discernable genetic disorder such as Down's syndrome is present, naming a disorder can be risky. And predicting the future for the young child is equally risky. Many doctors realize this and make an effort to balance the reality of the situation without being overly optimistic or unduly pessimistic. In all fairness to doctors, this is difficult and requires a great deal of skill.

So often medical and psychological professionals will give minimum prognostications because they are afraid to raise parents' hopes too high or to be held accountable if the child does not reach the desired level. While this is understandable, I have heard too many stories of children who have achieved or accomplished far more than anyone ever thought possible. My own son is one. According to all of his psychological assessments, he should never have had the capability to read, but read he does. He is limited to signs and labels and first-grade-level sentences; but he does read. Another mother told me her doctor predicted that her son would never walk; but at age five he suddenly started taking steps—and progressed to normal walking.

If I could make a plea to physicians and psychologists it would be to ask them to listen to the parents' concerns and estimates of their child's ability. I know that many of these parents are in denial; but not all of them are. Some are simply crying out for help. I suspect some doctors are also in denial, and do not want to deal with the problem, hoping perhaps someone else will. This is neither ethical nor good medical practice; but I know it occurs. Parents need to be encouraged to continue searching for the doctor who will listen to their honest concerns.

Once parents have obtained a diagnosis, the next step is to obtain services, and the counselor can help by offering current information about those available in the community. A parent who must search for services alone can feel frustrated, because often, several calls must be made before the right agency is located.

THE CHILD WHO BECOMES DISABLED AFTER ILLNESS OR ACCIDENT

The third situation, in which a child develops an illness or is injured and becomes permanently disabled can, of course, occur at any age. I am including it here merely for the sake of organization, although it could have fit into other chapters of this book.

When this occurs, the elements of medical crisis intensify the grief. A child who was known for a time as a normal child is now a different person. Although all parents of children with disabilities go through the grief process, this one has a slightly different element because the child functioned for a time in a normal fashion. Then the family was suddenly plunged into an entirely different scenario, much like the shock felt by the parents of the baby who is born with a disability. These parents will have all of the same experiences of the parents in the other scenarios, beginning when they receive the diagnosis.

THE CHILD WITH UNDIAGNOSED SYMPTOMS

The fourth condition is the most puzzling to parents. This child has delays in some areas that lead the parents to wonder if something may be wrong; but in general, the child is coping at a par with his or her peers, except for these few areas. Most often, these are the children who will be diagnosed as having learning disabilities once school begins.

Parents will find it difficult to describe some of the ways these children lag behind their peers. They may realize that the child has a very limited vocabulary, or they may see their child as immature in social behavior compared with other children. Or the child may be described as "difficult" to raise—fussy, not sleeping well, or a picky eater. If there is ADHD (Attention-Deficit Hyperactivity Disorder) this child may run the nursery-school teacher (and his parents) ragged. This may be the child who is labeled as "trouble" or "a handful" by everyone in the church nursery. Unfortunately, diagnosis for this child often does not occur until he or she is unable to cope with learning tasks in school.

No matter when the initial diagnosis is made—at birth, in the toddler years, or later—it is still a crisis. Crisis periods for families of children with disabilities are most likely to occur at the time of diagnosis, when the child begins to walk and talk, at the beginning of public-school attendance, and when the child reaches the age of legal majority, which often coincides with the time of leaving public school.[2]

SOURCES OF STRESS FOR PARENTS

Developmental Stages

As previously mentioned, the child's failure or slowness to reach the milestones of developmental growth are a source of stress for parents, and can produce a crisis. The child who does not perform tasks "on time" may become a scapegoat, and possibly be the target of abuse when he or she is labeled by the family as slow or retarded. The delay in reaching a milestone may cause the parents to seek medical help, where they are faced with the crisis of diagnosis.

If the diagnosis has already been made, seeing the months pass without the child accomplishing normal tasks brings further sadness. When the baby book has spaces to record the "firsts," and the spaces remain blank, parents become discouraged. Naturally, when children are severely disabled or so seriously ill that the prognosis for a normal life span is negative, parents will be even more affected by these markers of normal development as they realize their child may never attain them.

Involvement with Programs

Infant stimulation programs usually are structured so that the parent brings the child to the program and stays for some part of the activities, or the program occurs in the child's home with individual assistance from a social worker or teacher. Many states are now beginning public-school programs for children two years old, and these children are transported by the school system. It can be very difficult for a parent to put that child on a school bus and to be away from him or her for part of the day. (These programs are usually a half-day until age five or six.) The parent may worry about the child being able to communicate his or her needs, or about a long bus ride, especially for young children who require a wheelchair or a special seat.

Thus, parents with children in these programs will have another set of stressors in their lives. In addition to concerns about the bus ride, there is the pressure of getting a small child ready for school every day at the same time. Depending upon the child's disability and the age of the other children in the household, this can become a major orchestration. Half-day programs for preschoolers present additional problems involving care or transportation if both parents are working. Some cities may have after-school care that will accept preschoolers; but, in general, transportation to and from these programs is not included. On the other hand, a half-day program may be a godsend to the parent who does not work outside the home, and who then, at least, has a few hours every morning without the child.

Finding a reliable baby-sitter for the more active toddler who is developmentally delayed is another problem parents face. More skills are needed to care for a child who does not communicate well, who may require special care. Respite services operating in some cities can sometimes provide trained baby-sitters, but these are usually limited in the number of hours that can be used by each family per month. Time away, even for a movie and dinner out, must be carefully planned, because these sitters stay booked. I have had to arrange as far as three weeks in advance for a single evening out.

PARENTAL EXPERIENCES

Much of the research focuses on families who have toddlers with disabilities that were discovered at birth.[3] This occurs because many children have been in some kind of younger-age program, either for assessment or preschool, and were therefore available. In the past, research centered on the mother and child.[4] Only in recent years have studies been conducted which included fathers,[5] and only in the past few years has there been research that included siblings[6] and grandparents,[7] and this is limited. Often studies used small samples and focused on specific disabilities, so the results were not generally applicable to counseling.[8]

Several books discuss the research and offer valuable information for both parents and professionals.[9] Of equal value to the counselor, however, is knowledge of the parents' feelings about their situation. Some examples of these feelings are expressed in the following statements by preschoolers' parents or parents of older children as they reflected on those preschool years:

"Having a handicapped child permeates your life forever. Everything is changed—going shopping, finding time to read the newspaper or take a bath, relationships of family and friends—you name it."[10]

"There is a bad strain on our marriage because of our debts and my not being able to keep a job unless we find a program for Jessica."[11]

"Sometimes I feel like giving up—like I can't make one more phone call or write one more letter."[12]

"I want my life back."[13]

"I think professional counseling would have helped . . . had we been able to go to someone and say here's our problem and here's what's happening . . . it sure would help if someone could sort of guide us through a few steps."[14]

"I'd get up in the morning or go to bed at night and I'd ask, when is the heartache and pain going to leave? I accept now that Lisa will have Down syndrome all her life. . . . It's mentally and emotionally draining."[15]

"I think the grieving process takes on different forms all the time."[16]

"It was so helpful for me to get to know other parents . . . I found I could talk about 'bad' feelings toward my disabled son, and they had similar feelings. . . . We helped each other and cried together and took our kids out together. . . . That really helped."[17]

My own experience included all of these feelings. I also felt very isolated during those years. Twenty years ago, and perhaps still today in some areas, preschool programs were difficult to find. Federal Law PL 99–457, which extends the range of ages eligible for services, will eventually provide for preschool programs in all states.

All programs should have a means to allow parents to give input, and a design that will include a support group for parents. The counselor can assist the parent with beginning this support group if one is not available through the selected program. This is such a crucial need that it should not be overlooked.

The parent of a preschool child can spend a lot of hours alone with the child, and as a result, can become more and more isolated. If the child enters public school, it may be up to the parents again to form a support group if parenting needs and concerns are not addressed by the school. Most schools have PTAs and parent meetings of some sort, but very often these are for information or programmatic concerns only, and do not address the issues and needs of parents and families.

APPLICATION OF THE AFA

The Event

Several situations can lead a family into counseling when the child with a disability is in the toddler years. It could be that the parents are perceiving that something is wrong with their child, but they do not know how to proceed. Or the parents may have recently received a diagnosis on the child and are beginning the process of adjusting to being a different type of family, and of entering the world of those with disabilities. Or parents who had already had a diagnosis on their child may have received new testing results, changing the prognosis. This is especially distressing if medical problems involve a lesser quality of life, a shortened life expectancy, or if further surgical procedures are indicated.

Each possibility in the wide range of presenting problems calls for a different type of intervention. The counselor needs to know as much as possible about the exact nature of the child's disability and the family's circumstances. In some cases parents will need counseling so they can first settle their own emotional issues and then muster enough energy to deal with the problem. In other cases, specific referrals for community services should be made.

A child may be entering a new program with which the parents are dissatisfied, and they look to the counselor for help in dealing with the program providers and expressing their concerns. Perhaps the child's program participation complicates problems regarding the parents' work or transportation needs, with resulting feelings of frustration. Or there may be some consideration of a residential placement if a day placement is not suitable for the child or places too many demands on the parents. If this choice is made, it can be a source of great anxiety and guilt for parents.

Parents may seek counseling when they are expecting another child and are apprehensive because they do not know the cause of the existing child's disability. They may want information on genetic testing. Or they may know the probability of having another child with the same genetic disorder and may even be struggling with thoughts of an abortion.

Parents also may come to a counselor for help when they have no specific, identifiable complaint except that they feel overwhelmed. One parent may be suffering depression. Or they may not have been able to sort out the components of their lives, and everything looks hopeless as a result.

Parents may need some very practical help with behaviors they do not know how to control, such as temper tantrums or aggression toward a younger child. The child may be uncooperative while being bathed and dressed; he or she may resist potty training, or may not be interested in learning self-feeding. Parents may not know how to discipline a child who does not understand, but who needs limits to ensure his or her own safety or proper behavior.

Resources

Support by others is a crucial family resource. Mothers caring for children with disabilities can feel constantly exhausted, especially if the children have critical medical needs or exhibit hyperactivity. Another problem is that of the child who needs constant monitoring and care.

Family Definition of the Event

At this stage, the family may still be struggling with the "Why?" questions: "Why us? Why our child?" The parents may not yet be able to use their faith in God as a resource because they are still attempting to make sense of their situation, or they view the child's condition as their punishment for past transgressions. This may hinder their ability to establish support and seek services. They may be bitter and resentful, and then have problems dealing with those people in the community who could be of help. The bitterness may carry over into destructive patterns in spousal, extended family, and work relationships.

Amid these problems one parent may disengage, and the other will carry the responsibility for seeking help, meeting the child's physical needs, and teaching the child during the hours that the child is home. The parent who chooses not to cope with this will spend more time in other activities, such as increased work hours or a hobby, allowing the other parent to assume the bulk of the responsibility.

Readiness

The family needs to understand that it can begin to plan and prepare for the future. In the toddler years, the parents assume that preschool eventually will lead to all-day school. They need to realize that preschool children with disabilities are listed as "developmentally delayed," but when they are in an all-day situation at age six they will probably receive a different classification according to PL 94–142. They also can make plans for themselves, because having the child in school all day will give the primary caregiver more time.

It is difficult for parents of children in the preschool years to comprehend the future. To them it seems as though the children will be young forever. Parents often are so relieved at finding a placement for the child that they want to just breathe a sigh of relief and view this as a period of respite from struggles and hassles. It would be helpful, while allowing parents this "time off," to eventually lead them through some projections of where they see their child at certain points in the future. From this can come descriptions of possible future situations, and a list of what would be necessary to accomplish their desires for their child, themselves, and their other children.

It is never too early to seek information about a child's future. With this in mind, Appendix II contains references to Christian and secular organizations that provide information and support for parents.

Parents should also realize that their plans must always be accompanied by alternatives. Many situations involving the child are dependent upon the availability of services. Laws, funding, program priorities, and initiatives can and do change, and it will never be possible to completely and accurately predict a future course for any child.

Tuition increases, changes in policy, waiting lists for services, overcrowding of facilities, termination of staff, and hiring freezes can all affect placement of children in programs. As these situations occur, the life of the family is directly affected by other persons' determinations in which the family has had little or no input. This can cause feelings of helplessness, and loss of control over the family members' lives. And these feelings, in turn, can result in anger, frustration, and bitterness.

To keep a healthy state of mind in all of this requires a mixture of faith and common sense. The family has to walk the fine line of preparation and flexibility as plans and preparations are made—and changed. Faith is built by the realization that God does make provision for the child each step of the way; the key is in the parents' being yielded to God to allow that provision to occur. The counselor can encourage parents to seek God together in prayer, and also in a daily time of reading Scripture and/or inspirational writings. Even parents who feel overburdened with care of the child can find fifteen minutes a day for some time with the Lord. Being in concert with God's leading while simultaneously paying attention to what is occurring around them will keep parents from feeling beaten down, frustrated, defeated by the system, and victimized by circumstances.

A counselor can help restore a sense of control to the parents who feel that much of what has already happened to them and to their child has not been of their own doing. These feelings may intensify as they put themselves into a position of relying on others for care, support, information, schooling, and whatever they need for their child. During these processes, they will have to sort through opinions from others, many of which will be negative. And along with a sense of control over their child's placement and treatments, the counselor should help parents find and hold on to something else: hope.

COUNSELING IMPLICATIONS

The preschool years are crucial ones for the family of a child with disabilities. This is a time when parents must deal with a child who does not grow out of babyhood as other children do. It is also a time when parents find themselves almost immersed in various systems to receive necessary services for their child. They must, at the same time, deal with the issues related to the growth and change of their other children and perhaps their own adult lives, including their careers. The feeling of being a parent of a child with a disability and the subsequent acceptance or rejection of all that role includes grow sharper as the child becomes more visible to the public, no longer hidden in the wrappings of an infant.

The counselor needs to be aware of many things that often happen during this stage. The temptation may be to focus on the parents only in their role as parents of a child with a disability. Instead, counselors should consider the parents holistically as individuals who are coping with a particular situation, which happens to be a child with a disability. Parents do not wish to be viewed as abnormalities or objects of pity, but as any other people who have a problem situation.

Ideally, the counselor and parents will function as a team with a commitment to mutual growth in wisdom, understanding, and grace from God. They should show mutual respect for each other's knowledge, skills, and emotions, knowing that God will speak to each with words for themselves and for each other.

CHAPTER FIVE

THE SCHOOL YEARS

FOR MANY YEARS, ON THE FIRST DAY OF SCHOOL, I took a picture of my four children standing together at the front door of our house, sporting new lunchboxes and fresh haircuts. I remember the mixture of relief and apprehension I felt each year as they walked down the street to the bus stop—relief that the demands of summer childcare were over and apprehension about how Chris would relate to his new teachers. He did very well with some teachers, and I always hoped he would have them again.

And just as the beginning of the first day is an emotion-laden time, the end of that day can also be reassuring—or worrisome. Parents are eager, at the end of that first day, to hear their children's impressions of the new school year. But children with disabilities may never be able to tell their parents anything about the first day—or any other days. They may not be able to speak; and if they can speak, they may not be able to remember.

Parents may not be able to get information from the school as quickly as they would like, either. The school would not contact me until October of each school year regarding Chris's IEP (Individualized Education Plan) for the remainder of the year. And just as I felt relief that another school year had begun, I also was saddened to realize that each September was one year closer to the end of Chris's time in public education.

THE SPECIAL EDUCATION SCENE

Counselors who are aware of the problems of children in special education are more likely to be of genuine help to the family. Understanding the obstacles that parents often face adds a dimension to the counselor's level of empathy. And a practical working knowledge of the system enables the counselor to help the family develop effective strategies.

Special education in this country is anything but uniform. Although we have had PL 94–142, the Education for All Handicapped Children Act, since 1975, great diversity still occurs in its implementation. This is underscored by the results of a five-year collaborative study of children with special needs which was published recently by the Robert Wood Johnson Foundation. The study showed:

- The population of children in special education is extremely diverse, and includes large numbers of children categorized as learning disabled or speech impaired. Other classifications are emotionally disturbed, mentally retarded, blind, deaf, physically handicapped, chronically ill, or multiply handicapped. Some of these labels differ across states or cities.
- By far, most students in special education are mainstreamed; that is, they attend regular schools and are spending at least part of their day in a regular class.
- Once a child is determined to be eligible to receive services, categorization and placement differs widely across states and cities.
- Only 29 percent of children with special needs were diagnosed before age five.
- Usually less than half of all parents attended their children's IEP meeting.

- Boys in special education outnumber girls approximately two to one. This is found most in children labeled as speech impaired, learning disabled, emotionally disturbed, and mentally retarded.
- Only about 10 percent of all families of special education students received any kind of psychological counseling.
- Twenty-eight percent of all families of special education students reported that the disability of their child had caused stressful effects on major areas of their lives, including jobs, friendships, and marriages.[1]

VIEWING EACH FAMILY AS UNIQUE

Children with disabilities differ more from each other than they differ from nondisabled children. Also, there are greater differences among families who have children with disabilities than there are between those families and families with nondisabled children.[2] It is those individual differences that the counselor must always consider. In contrast, some counselors may overgeneralize and categorize these families, prematurely judging them all as having the same problems. As one counselor said in a family therapy session, "Well, you know, families with handicapped children . . .", implying that that was probably a major cause of the family's problem, without looking for other possibilities. While all these parents share some general concerns, counselors must refrain from making the assumption that all parents have certain characteristics, and certain problems, they acquire because of their child's disability.

Not all families with children with disabilities have problems attributable directly to the child's disability. However, all families will have to cope with the situation, and how they cope is dependent upon a number of factors such as educational level, financial and other resources, spiritual level, marital stability, number and ages of siblings, and disability, gender, and age of the child—in other words, on the unique factors of the individuals involved. There is no such thing as a "Parents of a Special-Needs Child Syndrome."

THE NATURE OF THE SCHOOL SYSTEM

Virtually all parents will have to cope with a school system in some form, and most often this will be the public schools. Even children who are placed in residential settings must have their paperwork done through public schools, unless it is a placement that the parents, themselves, arrange and completely finance. The cost of residential care is so high that very few parents can afford to act in such an autonomous manner.

Each parent's interaction with a school is unique, depending upon the nature of the system and the specific personnel involved. Sometimes confusion results because the school system must abide by federal, state, and local ordinances which may not always be in harmony with one another.

Sources of Tension for Parents

Tensions are inherent in the world of special education. One of the first sources of this tension is the process of evaluation of the child for placement in special education classes. If the child is already in school, he or she must, according to regulations, remain in his or her current classroom situation until the evaluation process is complete. The child may be experiencing continuing learning and/or behavioral problems during this time. By law, this process can take no longer than sixty-five administrative working days, from referral to eligibility determination.

There are six formal assessment components for a child—educational, medical, sociocultural, psychological, developmental, and "other," such as speech or language. All of these assessments require time to compile the appropriate information. Some might require money, too, unless the school system offers to provide medical evaluations to ease the financial burden of the parent. When parents do not agree with results of the assessments conducted by the school system, they may have the added cost of a private assessment. which is conducted at their expense.

Another source of tension occurs when the process is complete and the child receives a classification—in effect, a label, to receive services. While this step may signify the start of much-needed assistance, it also can be stigmatizing for both the child and the parents. This label probably will remain with the child all through his or her school years, continually presenting the possibility for problems with his or her self-esteem.

Tensions may also occur once the child is placed in a program if parents and the school have widely divergent viewpoints as to what is required to meet the child's needs. A case in point is the enthusiastic, first-year teacher, well meaning and sincere in her work, who taught a class in independent living skills. The IEP for her students included setting the table. However, in her enthusiasm, she insisted that her students set the table with salad and dinner forks, bread and butter plates, salad plates, water and beverage glasses, and dessert spoon and fork above the dinner plate, in the British style. Most parents would have been happy with knife and spoon to the right of the plate and fork and napkin to the left. Setting such unrealistic goals for students results in report cards that always have "IP" (In Progress), instead of "M" (Mastered), in learning these skills.

The intent of PL 94–142 is that children's individual needs be met by assessing the child and then providing the services that are needed. Unfortunately, however, what may occur in practice is that the school system establishes programs, assesses children, and then decides who fits into which slots. (Unfortunately, this practice often continues when the child has finished school and is in community services.) Making the child fit the system may be another source of tension between parents and the school. This is sometimes intensified by budget considerations which often drive program provision, requiring parents to deal with limits on services.

PARENTAL INTERACTION WITH FORMAL SYSTEMS

A second source of tension, especially for the 28 percent of children who are diagnosed before age five, is that the family has been inter- acting with formal systems, such as medical personnel, preschools, and agencies, long before other parents, whose interactions with formal systems regarding their children usually begin with public-school enrollment. Therefore, once the child is enrolled in school, the parent may wish to decrease his or her involvement with formal systems— to take some "time off."[3] However, the intent of PL 94–142 is for the child's IEP to be developed with parental involvement. One of four situations results as parents choose to be uninvolved, minimally involved, cooperative, or adversarial regarding their child's IEP.

The Uninvolved Parent

The first situation is that the parent remains absent from interac- tions involving the school. As was mentioned earlier, about half of the parents never attend their children's IEP meeting. Some of these probably sign the IEP when it is sent home with the child and return it to school the same way. Some parents never sign it at all, in which case the child then cannot receive services unless school personnel make a greater effort to contact those parents, perhaps even making a home visit. Because of this problem, some states are devising initiatives to allow the child to receive services without parental signature, a well-intentioned plan which allows children to receive services, but also has the negative effect of decreasing parental input.

The Minimally Involved Parent

Another fairly common occurrence is for the parent to attend the IEP meeting and sign whatever plan the school has written out. Parents may be so glad for their child to have a placement that they will not ask any questions or make any demands upon the school, either for fear of jeopardizing that placement or because they do not know what it is that they can demand. It is also highly unlikely that these parents will initiate any further conferences during the year.

The Vocal Parent

The third and fourth situations are comprised of the smallest group of parents, those who are often seen as problems to the school system, because they are the most vocal. These parents want to be actively involved in planning their child's education and will offer their observations, experiences, and insight. They also know their children's rights under PL 94–142, and can be cooperative (the third situation) or adversarial (the fourth situation). Unfortunately, both kinds of parents may be seen as troublesome to the system because they are often requesting change. This is especially true when the school is a closed system which does not like to open its boundaries to "nonprofessionals," even if these parents are professionals in other fields.

On the other hand, the school may welcome parents and view them as partners in providing an education for the children. The ideal situation is when parents, teachers, and administrators work together for the best interests of the child. Sometimes, however, knowledgeable and caring parents fail to grasp the realities and limits of the school system, and make unreasonable demands. As mentioned in the previous chapter, counselors can assist parents in developing those skills that will allow for negotiation and produce results for the benefit of the child and the family as a whole, while recognizing the limits of reality.

PARENTAL CONCERNS

Every September, parents of children with disabilities take on a recurring role as their children's educational advocate. For some parents, this advocacy becomes almost an occupation. And as noted earlier, parents who are most involved with their child's education are the ones who will experience the most conflicts. However, these conflicts may be seen as worth the price as parents recognize that change will only come about when consumer demand is great enough. Laws such as PL 94–142 and PL 99–457 were passed because of parents' demands. Parents' continued awareness and participation are crucial in assuring the enforcement of the spirit and intent of those laws.

The parent of a school-aged child who has no problems may have no idea of the energy required of a parent whose child is in special education. Sometimes the process seems designed to wear parents down. The following list is by no means complete, but it reflects the more common situations that I have experienced or have had related to me by parents and teachers:

- Many students who are mainstreamed are put into classes in which neither the teachers nor other students are informed as to the needs of the child, resulting in undesirable situations. A time of preparation for everyone involved would go a long way toward everyone's benefiting from the experience.
- Parent-teacher conferences are often set up during school hours, which may be during a parent's work day.
- New teachers, while having all the right intentions and being dedicated to the children, may not understand parents' feelings of care and concern for their children. These teachers may feel uncomfortable with assertive parents and view them as threats.
- Parents may forget that their child is not the only one in the class. Even though class size in special education is small, parents must realize the teacher has a demanding job.
- The IEP meeting, by law, must have both the teacher and an administrator present with the parent(s). Often, other persons who serve the child, such as physical therapists, occupational therapists, speech therapists, physical education teachers, and others will also be present. In this setting, the parent who requests information or changes in the IEP may feel that he or she is on trial. A room full of professionals and one parent can

be an intimidating situation. But meetings in special education and in community services continue to be held in this manner.

- When the child is unable to communicate about the day at school because of his or her young age or disability, the parents are dependent upon the teacher for input. This input is especially important for parents who feel they do not have control over their child while he or she is in school. These feelings may be intensified if the child is very dependent upon the parents for meeting his or her needs.

- Parents can become frustrated with the entire process of placement and IEP changes. There is a paperwork jungle that occurs and, while there are federal regulations that stipulate certain time lines be met, there are often delays beyond the time lines for one reason or the other.

- Parents who have been unsuccessful advocates for their school children may take a "What's the use?" attitude and choose not to be involved.

- A child who is labeled in "special education" and is not enrolled in enough mainstream courses in junior and senior high school does not receive a diploma but a "certificate of attendance." This is a hindrance for the post-high-school adult who has sufficient ability to get an entry-level job. If he or she becomes aware of this situation while still in school, one of two things will happen. The student may be motivated, and, if he or she has the ability to do so, will work harder so as to be able to take regular classes and get the diploma. On the other hand the student who does not have the ability will have to stay in self-contained classes, and may then give up on learning at all, knowing there will never be a diploma.

- Parents also feel labeled by the system—lumped together in a group, and categorized by their child's disability.

- Parents who move from one system to another may find vast differences. Sometimes these differences begin with delays in getting their child enrolled in special education in the new school system, even though they hand-carry the current IEP to the new school. This is a particular concern to parents affected by military or corporate moves. Some families may be so dissatisfied with one system that they move to another city or school district to get better services.

HELPING FAMILIES MEET SPECIFIC NEEDS

Because ages of children in school can range from five to twenty-two, I will not address use of the AFA here in the same manner as I did in previous chapters, which were more age-specific. Instead, I will focus on two specific areas in which parents of school-age children with disabilities seek help: the behavior of their children and obtaining needed services for them from schools and other agencies.

At the risk of being repetitive, the first task of the counselor is to determine the family's level of functioning, as well as its needs and resources. This can be accomplished by use of the AFA.

Helping Parents Deal with Children's Behaviors

Family therapists will often view a child's behavioral problems as an observable signal, unconscious on the child's part, of a dysfunction in the family system. In some cases the child's behavior is either an attempt to take the focus off the marital conflict or a cry for help in a non-nurturing or abusive family. It can also reflect a crisis situation in the family. None of these factors should be discounted automatically when a family comes for help because of behavior problems with a child who has a disability.

However, very often this family experiences behavioral difficulties because the parents simply do not know how to train and discipline their child with a disability. Perhaps discipline techniques that worked with their other children do not work with this child, and they are frustrated. Or this child may have behaviors they never saw in their other children, and they feel defeated in dealing with them. They may be so used to being the child's constant caregivers that they become, inadvertently, overindulgent until one day they realize their child is beyond their control. These problems of behavior are likely to intensify as the child becomes older and physically larger, and thus harder to handle.

Being unable to cope with the behavior of this child does not mean these are inadequate, unintelligent, or uncaring parents. It does mean that they are likely to be frustrated, puzzled, confused, and perhaps angry. The following example may demonstrate how these parents may feel when confronted by a behavior problem they cannot handle.

Suppose your morning newspaper were printed in Chinese and you were expected to gather information from the paper and process it with no knowledge of that language. Without a translation manual and guidelines, you would feel helpless and stupid, especially if others automatically expected you to accomplish this task. If no help were available, you would probably figure out what little you could from the pictures in the newspaper and give up on the rest. This is how parents feel when they have exhausted their knowledge in dealing with their child and find themselves in an unfamiliar situation.

Help is available in many forms for parents who need assistance in dealing with the behavior problems of a child with a disability. Choice of a strategy to effect change depends upon the age of the child, the type of disability, and the nature of the problem. Despite these individual considerations, however, the overall strategy that seems to work best is some type of a behavioral approach. This is the method most classroom teachers, especially special education teachers, find successful in both maintaining discipline and encouraging learning. It is also used as an effective behavior approach by families who have young children without disabilities. Because younger children think in concrete terms, rewards and positive reinforcers they can see, understand, and directly connect to their behavior lead them to make behavioral change.

Where appropriate, a similar system works with children with disabilities. Patience is imperative, however, because for some children, particularly those with mental disabilities, the behavioral changes occur over long periods of time. The greater the impairment, the longer the process. Parents of these children must be consistent for much longer periods of time; and because little progress may be seen at first, they may become discouraged. There is, however, a payoff in the long run.

Some communities have classes for parents to learn these skills. Others have specialists who will come into the home, design a program, model its use, and make weekly visits to follow up and support the parents.

I have seen such a program in action with a mother and son, whom I will call Janet and Michael. Michael was a bright, charming seven-year-old who had Down's syndrome. I met him and his mother when we gathered at a bus stop for summer day camp for the children. Michael kept running away from his mother, not just at the bus stop, but wherever they went, making life very difficult for Janet. Michael was large for his age, which made holding on to his hand impossible when he was determined to take off. Janet contacted the local office for mental retardation services and asked for a family trainer to help her with this problem.

Susan, the trainer, began the program by observing Michael at home and in other settings and then setting up rewards and consequences for his behavior. Susan accompanied Michael and Janet to the bus stop several times and reinforced Michael for positive behavior. Susan also made home visits to help Janet with some of Michael's other behaviors. By the end of the summer, when Michael would begin to take off, Janet would say, "You may not run," the same phrase she had used consistently all summer. It helped her son to remember to stay put and wait for the bus.

I have used similar tactics with Chris. Because he operated at a lower level than Michael, the program took much longer; but it, too, had its rewards. I had a problem with Chris getting off the school bus in front of our house and then going elsewhere in the neighborhood, either to a friend's house to see if the children were home yet or to watch an exciting event, such as a lawn being mowed or a tree being felled. I began by meeting him at the bus and leading him into the house, helping him to hang up his jacket, telling him to use the bathroom and wash his hands, and then putting out his after-school snack—the built-in reward.

This process took about two school years for satisfactory mastery, that is, for him to do the entire process without any verbal prompts from me. He then progressed to getting off the bus a block away from our house, at the regular stop, and going through his whole routine independently, including fixing his own snack. In the process, he gained independence, as well as pride in himself; and I gained some peace of mind. These may sound like long, drawn-out experiences; but behavioral training is just that. Each objective, step, and reinforcer must be clearly planned and then used consistently until the desired behavior is achieved. After that, intermittent reinforcers, such as praise, will usually maintain the behavior.

Children with disabilities, including those problems that are not readily visible or are not usually considered to be a disability, such as Attention Deficit Disorder, often lack a sense of internal structure. Giving them a sense of organization and routine helps them make sense of their world and adds to their feelings of security and positive self-esteem. When a child has a physical disability only without any accompanying cognitive impairment, the use of behavioral techniques helps the young child as it would any other child without a disability. As this child grows older, some other type of behavioral program may be beneficial to encourage continued therapy or learning of skills. This type of child may even be motivated to help design the program.

In all children, the goal of behavior strategies is that the child will become self-motivated, and structure and controls will come from within, as much as is possible.

Helping Families Help Children Learn Skills

Skills training is basic to most children with disabilities, except perhaps those who are most severely impaired and without any motor function or cognitive awareness. With modern computers and communication boards, even those who appear most severely disabled today can be taught skills, including skills needed to become wage earners.

Parents often need assistance in helping their children develop specific self-help or educational skills. An example of self-help skills is learning to dress. Most parents with a toddler know how to teach the child to lay out a jacket on the floor, upside down, so that the child can insert his or her arms, flip the jacket over the head, and therefore always put it on correctly.

More difficult is the fine motor skills required to zip or button the jacket. (While Velcro has made life simpler for those with disabilities, the child must still learn how to line up the two pieces of Velcro.) These skills can be taught by backward chaining. In this process, the parent does the whole operation for the child—except the very last step, such as pulling the zipper all the way up, which the child completes. The next time, the child does a little bit more of the last step, and so on, until he or she can do the entire procedure. This type of teaching has a built-in reward, because the child is always successful. It can be applied to everything from learning to dress to making sandwiches.

Parents may experience particular feelings of inadequacy and frustration in helping children develop educational skills. They may identify with their child's frustration over learning difficulties and then be ineffective because they are caught up in the emotion of the child. A parent needs to learn how to take the child through the process required, and to reinforce what is being done in school.

Realistic expectations for this child and knowing how long each day to reasonably spend on the work are basic necessities of this training.

Parents do not need to have college classes in teaching to be effective helpers of their children. What they do need is encouragement and direction. Teachers are usually delighted to assist parents who want to help their children at home. Counselors can assist parents by helping them avoid guilt for the child's learning problems and by encouraging them to accept the child as he or she is. As parents learn to accept themselves as being created by God for a purpose, despite their own flaws and failings, they will also be able to accept their child in the same manner. They will then be able to convey both God's love and their own unconditional love to the child.

PARENTS AS ADVOCATES

Parents of children with disabilities need skills to deal with service providers in schools, public agencies, or medical facilities. These skills will be useful all their lives, because they will always be dealing with a formal system of one type or another. Children who have physical disabilities only and, to some extent, those with mild, cognitive impairment, can learn to be their own advocates as they reach adulthood. Parental involvement in advocacy for the adult with a disability will depend upon the adult child's level of independence.

Parents should be encouraged in their advocacy efforts, because those who make fewer attempts to stay involved sometimes quit the effort entirely, becoming burned out, isolated, and out of touch with the community. This leads to a sense of helplessness.[4]

I am cautious about making absolute statements, but I offer one here based on many years of experience. Parents of children with special needs *never* have too much information. It is their most powerful asset, especially in their role as advocates, and can be obtained in many ways. Parent training centers comprise one valuable resource. Many regional centers across the United States offer parent training that is specific to special education. These Parent Training and Information Centers (PTIC) are provided under PL 98–199, a 1983 amendment to PL 94–142.

I am familiar with the Parent Educational Advocacy Training Center (PEATC) in Alexandria, Virginia. It has spawned Parent Resource Centers in local school districts. Each is staffed by both a school professional and a parent resource person who is neither a teacher nor an administrator, but is, ideally, the parent of a child in special education. While PEATC trains the trainers, the local Parent Resource Centers train parents in legislation that affects special education, student and parental rights, and advocacy.[5] See Appendix II for more information about Parent Training and Information Centers and other sources of information, such as state and federal offices, national organizations, parent and consumer groups, and parent coalitions.

Empowering Parents to Advocate

While some knowledge of the school process is valuable for counselors to help parents with school-related problems, it is also crucial for the counselor to be aware of the feelings of parents regarding the process.

When asked to indicate feelings experienced when meeting with school personnel, parents most often responded with these words: "inadequate, exhausted, intimidated, hopeful, fearful, confused, tentative, worried, anxious, challenged." When teachers were asked to identify feelings experienced at parent-teacher conferences, their responses were "sure, capable, confident, energetic, calm, helpful, adequate and knowledgeable." [6]

Counselors can use several ideas to help parents move to a position of feeling as the teachers do. Allen Ivey's model of client developmental levels and counseling styles[7] can be helpful in preparing parents to deal with school problems. While use of the AFA will aid the counselor in obtaining an overall picture of family functioning, it must be noted that "clients exhibit different developmental levels as they talk about different topics or issues."[8] The counselor, then, must be able to shift styles to accommodate these differing levels. People who are functioning well in most areas can get "stuck" on one topic and may need a different style of counseling to move them out of that "stuckness," a word introduced by Fritz Perls to denote a sense of immobility or an impasse.

The Four Developmental Levels of Functioning

A parent at the first, or D–1 level, requires a directive approach.[9] This may include basic instruction or a knowledgeable person to accompany the parent to the IEP meeting. This parent will probably make statements like, "I can't talk to the teacher," "I just don t know what to do," or "I get flustered."

A parent at the D–2 level will be more motivated, and probably will have made some prior attempts to get information and/or to make changes, but may have been unsuccessful. Ivey recommends assertiveness training, cognitive behavior modification, and reality therapy for people at this level.[10] This parent may make statements such as "I went in and let the principal have it," or "I told them they were all wrong," or "How do I get through to those people?" or "They don't seem to understand how I feel about this." This person will benefit by a coaching style of counseling, and by information.

A parent at the D–3 level is one who has the knowledge, information, and skills for advocacy but needs some help in sorting out the situation. Ivey recommends primarily the use of attending skills.[11] This parent may be wrestling with deeper issues of not only wanting to get his or her own child's needs met, but also of working to make changes in the system as a whole. He or she may be thinking through the meaning of these issues to self and family.

At the D–4 level, Ivey describes a self-starter who actually directs the counseling sessions.[12] This might include the client and the counselor who are working together to mutually learn and perhaps mutually advocate. In this situation, the counselor would need a strong interest and commitment to the issues involved.

Most parents will have school-related problems at the D-2 level. However, because people often are at different levels on different topics, the counselor will need to be alert and be able to shift styles for topics as needed.

The Development of the System

In a way, the parents and professionals in special education progress through these same developmental levels in the provision of programs as we have just examined as applying to the family. The first phase was legislation, the second the establishment of programs, the third a phase of learning about each other, and now it is time for mutual learning, with each respecting the other's field of expertise and growing together. I like this statement made by one parent advocate: "We parents are like tea bags—we don't know our own strength until we get into hot water. Professionals are now beginning to admire our strength and our coping mechanisms."[13]

I would encourage counselors to help parents of children with special needs to realize that they can be strengthened by and benefit from involvement in school. And that they can make a real difference, not only for their own child, but for other children as well.

CHAPTER SIX

TRANSITIONING:
THE SCHOOL BUS ISN'T COMING
ANY MORE

JUNE IS TRADITIONALLY THE MONTH of high-school proms, yearbooks, and graduations. Graduates are usually reminded that the word commencement means a beginning. I have watched three of my four sons participate in graduation ceremonies. One went on to college, a bachelor's degree, and then marriage. One is currently in college. One is in a residential training school. The first two boys had several options open to them and chose college. When the fourth graduates, he, too, will have several choices. The third, Chris, had very limited options and virtually no choice regarding his future.

Graduation from high school or completion of eligibility to remain in school can be a time of great stress or even of crisis to a family who has a young adult with a disability. A time which is normally filled with expectation and hope for the future can be one of turmoil, frustration, or despair for this family. Before my college-bound sons graduated from high school, we went to college nights, read dozens of brochures, and considered several options such as the military, community and local colleges, and colleges away from home. They also were able to apply in several places for jobs and to choose where they wanted to work for the summers.

This is the usual situation when a young adult finishes high school and is being launched into the world by the family. And in this "usual" situation, young adults have options about what to do with their lives.

Families who have young adults with disabilities are in a different position, however. The most striking difference is that there are few, if any, choices for these young people. What they will do after high school is dictated by the services available in the community in which they live. It is also sometimes dependent upon their family's finances. Outside of SSI, little or nothing is available in the way of financial assistance. (And it seems ironic that SSI payments are one hundred dollars less when the young adult lives at home than when he or she lives away from home. With increased financial support or additional services, the family could conceivably keep the young adult at home, at an overall lower cost, both financial and emotional. I cannot speak to every case, but I know many young adults who are in less than ideal circumstances, in part because of this system.)

RESPONSIBILITY OF PARENTS

This burden on parents seems unfair. For example, the commonwealth of Virginia spends $55,000 to build one jail cell and $17,500 annually to maintain a prisoner; yet for parents who want to help their young adults with disabilities there is precious little. If those who are disabled and did nothing to cause their condition were allotted the same money the state gives to prisoners, who did make some choices to get where they were, parents would have nothing about which to complain. I realize that I am venturing into public policy and out of counseling, but this is an example of the frustration parents experience as they try to provide optimal situations for their children who are leaving special education programs.

Despite the nature of the young adult's disability, responsibility for the child's welfare falls, in varying degrees, to the parents. It is almost a sense of déjà vu—a repeat of the process to obtain school services that now is being replayed in another arena some fifteen years later.

Some Young Adults of Today

There has been an abundance of rhetoric about normalization and least restrictive environments for people with disabilities. However, in reality, the concept of normalization does not apply in most cases. It is not normal for a person to be forced to leave his or her home and community, no matter what the nature of the disability, and live elsewhere with strangers. On the radio, I heard a man of thirty-four testify to a Georgia commission that he had to live in an out-of-state nursing home, because he was a quadriplegic who required a ventilator to live, and no services were available to him in Georgia. He told of his loneliness away from family and friends and of the despair of living with elderly persons who were severely incapacitated.[1]

I know several young adults who have completed their schooling and now live in varying circumstances, described below. All of them are in their twenties. I have changed their names; their circumstances, however, are authentic.

- Danielle lives at home with her mother, who provides transportation to and from her part-time job and everywhere else, such as to Special Olympics events.
- Charles lives in an out-of-state group home.
- Tom is now living with his mother after she became dissatisfied with the level of care he was receiving in a group home.
- John's parents have invested money to purchase a home for John to share with two other residents and houseparents, who are salaried through the city.
- Richard lives at home with his retired parents who are his constant companions and who transport him to all activities and jobs when available.
- Paul lives in a nursing home for the elderly.
- Kate lives at home with her parents and is transported to recreation three times a week in a specially equipped mini van that's part of the city bus system. Her mother reports several problems with the bus service, however.
- Skip has been at home with his mother for over a year and has just obtained a job with transportation.

Most of the parents of these people would tell you that they are not satisfied with the current situations with their children.

Obstacles in the Community

A 1988 statewide conference, "Community Integration of Virginians with Developmental Disabilities," dealt with several issues that I have mentioned. The following statements recorded in the conference proceedings reflect the problems parents face.

- "All people with disabilities are entitled to the paid *supports* necessary to live in a *home in the community* and to *participate* in everyday community life."
- "People cannot choose where and with whom they live because funding is tied to specific program models and not the person."
- "People with severe disabilities are often considered 'ineligible' for community living arrangements (i.e., they do not meet the entrance criteria established by the local CSB [Community Services Board])."
- "There is a lack of available, flexible, individualized support services for people with severe disabilities to reside in their own home."
- "Case management is not available for many and inadequate for many other people with disabilities. . . ."
- "Persons with disabilities have limited choices in the type and location of employment activities."
- "Absence of available transportation hinders work opportunities. . . ."
- "There is a limited, statewide transition planning from school to work throughout the state."[2]

These problems are not limited to Virginia. In Ohio, families have formed a consortium to operate a group home for their daughters who are mildly mentally retarded because the state, with a waiting list of sixty-five hundred, did not know what to do.[3] In Pennsylvania, more than five thousand people are on waiting lists for services. Hundreds of people are living at home with no services.[4] A survey conducted in western Illinois showed that students completing school waited two years or more for services.[5] A federal study by the Rehabilitation Services Administration showed that needs of students with physical disabilities were not being met by school-to-work transitioning programs.[6]

Even if the young adult is successfully employed, other frustrations come into play. Normalization would imply that a person who was able to would work at a full-time job. However, the structure of SSI discourages full-time employment; the system is designed to keep people dependent.

Parents are chided by professionals for not actively pursuing increased wages and job responsibilities for their adult children with disabilities.[7] However, a recent study demonstrated that among people receiving SSI, the net disposable income was the same for those employed part time as it was for those employed full time, both at minimum-wage rates, which is usually the rate at which people with disabilities are hired.[8]

STRESS AND CRISIS IN THE FAMILY

The Event

It is critical that counselors understand these issues that parents of older children with disabilities face. One of them is stress, which becomes significantly higher in a family as the child with the disability becomes older,[9] and the normal, expected events in a family do not occur on time.[10] This family then is in a double bind. They are under stress having an older child with special needs; and now they have to face the reality that normal events in other families, and in their own family with their other children, will either not occur on time, or will not occur satisfactorily.

The parents' age and marital status also are considerations. Parents of a twenty-year-old child can be forty to sixty years old. In the past, most parents with children of this age were older, largely because of the birth of children who had Down syndrome relatively late in the parents' lives. Now, because of birth control and prenatal screening for older mothers, there are fewer older parents of these children in their twenties. More parents are in their forties, an age when it could be difficult to keep this young adult at home. Women in their forties are often working outside the home, or going back to school. Men in their forties are employed full time and usually very involved in their careers. Younger siblings may still be living at home—although, of course, this child could be a first, a middle, or a youngest, and the family's needs would differ accordingly. No matter what age the parents are, however, they are most likely caught in the middle of a situation in which demand for services has exceeded the supply. All of these possibilities can become even more complicated if the couple has divorced, and primary responsibility for the adult child with a disability is assigned to one parent. I'm especially aware of this now that my own marriage of twenty-five years has ended. Our new situation will certainly be a factor in planning for Chris's future.

While each individual's plight will be different depending on many factors that can be assessed by the AFA, the event will likely be one of the following circumstances:

1. The young adult can leave home but will need special assistance to do so successfully. Choices will be somewhat limited, depending on the nature of the disability and the goals.

2. The young adult can leave home, but the choices are severely limited to a few choices with only one option, or no choices at all. The parents will most likely remain involved with this person's care to some extent.

3. The parents would like the young adult to live at home and participate in the community but there are no opportunities and resources to do this.

4. The parents insist on keeping the young adult at home and remain the primary caregivers, whether or not other services are available.

The following discussion will offer a closer look at each of these specific family situations.

Leaving Home with Special Assistance. The first situation is most likely to occur when the young adult has a physical disability without cognitive impairment and wants to attend college or to live alone and find a nonprofessional job. Because of his or her physical limitation it may be easier to get into college, if the entrance requirements can be met, than to find a job. But both choices involve several challenges.

A young person with a physical disability has to address different concerns in choosing a college than does a nondisabled student. In addition to meeting the entrance requirements and having adequate finances for the college that meets the educational requirements for his or her selected field of study, the student may also need a special van, computer equipment, a personal care assistant, or an interpreter if he or she is hearing impaired or deaf. Those who have vision impairments may also require special equipment and transportation assistance. And when all these needs are arranged for, there are still the additional challenges most people take for granted, such as the accessibility of the dormitories, classrooms, libraries, and restrooms.

The student with learning disabilities also has special needs upon finishing the high-school years. Students' situations can be described by several categories. Due to the wide range in cognitive functioning, some students may have only received a certificate of attendance, some a high-school diploma, and some will have dropped out of school before completion. While schools pay a lot of attention to identification, evaluation, and placement of students with learning disabilities, there seems to be little concern with helping them transition to regular classes and attain a diploma.[11] Concomitantly, as in other disabilities, services are not sufficient for successful transition from school to work or further schooling, and vary widely from district to district. One large school system has only three vocational planners for a high-school population of over fifteen thousand students, while a neighboring system has a special vocational counselor in each of its five high schools.

Having Few Options. A great deal of tension and frustration can be present in the second situation when both the young adult and the parents desire a job and/or education and living situation outside of the home, but the options are severely limited or nonexistent. Parents will have to become actively involved in effecting some changes in this area.

The higher the level of functioning of the young adult, the more options the parents have to explore. The parents' own educational levels and financial resources also have a decided effect. As parents become more knowledgeable about how to obtain services, their options increase; and as they are financially able, they can provide services, such as a companion when needed, or transportation, or even purchase a home as John's parents did. Albert's family helped him get a fast-food-restaurant job, which he loved, and where he even earned raises. Unfortunately, Albert's family has since moved to another state because of his father's occupation, and no jobs are available there for Albert. His mother is now driving him to programs for recreation and some limited vocational training five days a week.

Desire to Remain at Home. In the third situation, the parents would like the young adult to remain at home, but no options exist. This was very much my situation, and it is directly related to funding. Earlier I noted the amount of money spent on prisoners, with very little, if any, return to society. In comparison, for every dollar spent on rehabilitation programs for the disabled in 1980, sixteen dollars were returned by the participants in wages earned, taxes paid, and other market-place activities.[12]

I read about a local program involving foster parents for disabled adults which trains people and pays them fifteen thousand dollars a year, plus annual vacation time, to care for a disabled adult in their home. Parents who care for their own disabled son or daughter receive a little over six thousand dollars in SSI per year, no vacation time, and little or no support. There is a tremendous inequity, indeed a vacuum, in supporting families who are caring for their own children with disabilities. Increased funding to assist these families in caring for their children at home would be of significant help. In addition, churches could provide volunteer services in this area. Chapter 10 explores these efforts in detail.

At Home But Without Plans. The last situation is one in which the parents keep their young adult at home and refuse to investigate any options. This is a parent's prerogative, but the dynamics require some examination. Is the young adult being taught self-help skills by being at home? Is there vocational training or a job? Are there any recreation and leisure activities? Does the young adult know other people of similar age and does he or she engage in activities with them? What will happen to this person if one or both of the parents becomes ill or dies? Who will be responsible to care for this person? Will the child suddenly be placed in an institution if this occurs?

Family Definition of the Event

Feelings of helplessness and being out of control are the most vexing and crisis-causing in families during this transitional time. For example, if I suddenly had to have Chris come back home to live with me, I would be in a real quandary. It would be extremely stressful for me, because I cannot quit working. I would be in crisis while scrambling for alternatives. Counselor and author Norm Wright speaks of his daughter's coming back home to live for a while after being out on her own. He has a son with a disability who was placed in a residential situation at age eleven; the same year, his daughter (who is not disabled) left home. Her move back home was difficult because he and his wife had, as he put it, "adjusted to the empty nest," and liked it.[13] He did not tell how the situation was resolved, but I can guess there was some stress, and a lot of readjustment.

A component of how the family defines the event, as well as part of the family's resources, is trust and faith in God. One of my central issues was concern for the future. For my son's first ten years I agonized over who would care for him when I was no longer here. I could not stand the thought of his being an abandoned adult. But, as I mentioned in the Introduction, the Lord gave me a beautiful gift of peace when I surrendered my life and all that was in it to him. I do not know now where Chris's next placement will be; but I do know that God knows and it will be for Chris's benefit. Along with every mother I talk to, I believe that no one can care for my child as I do. But that does not mean my child will not be okay if someone else has to do the caregiving.

I believe my parental duty is to investigate and plan as much as I can and to leave the rest to God. I have enrolled Chris in a community trust to provide for him when there is no longer a living parent. (See chapter 7 for more about such arrangements.) I have named guardians for that time. And I have been investigating the next possible step for him when his current placement expires. But I also realize that there are some variables I cannot control, and so I work on, taking charge of as much as I can.

Family Resources, and Residuals from Past Problems

When the family is at this stage, knowing how they have solved problems in the past will be essential for the counselor. This will be a clue as to the pattern of family functioning. Now is a time to focus on what has been leftover and unresolved in the past as well as to assess the family's strengths. By the time the child with a disability reaches age eighteen or twenty, the family members have been through a lot, steadily acquiring a variety of skills that have brought them this far. Even though they may yet have a lot to do, focusing on those strengths will give a foundational base from which to work.

Too often counselors at this point equate parents' statements of being satisfied or proud of their child with denial, sublimation, or overcompensation.[14] Parents should see positives in their situations, and counselors should encourage those feelings. In one study, parents and social workers were asked if parents had been made stronger by caring for a child with a disability. While 46 percent of the parents said they had been made stronger, only 9 percent of the social workers expected parents would feel that way. When asked if parents wanted to be encouraged to be strong, 67 percent said they did; but only 26 percent of the social workers believed that they did.[15]

I can identify with those parents who felt they had been made stronger by their experience, although I do not know what my life would have been like without my son. My values are probably very different than they would have been if none of my children had a disability. And my sons may have reflected those values, showing a compassion and understanding of others beyond what I saw in their young peers. Sibling research has confirmed that children who have brothers and sisters with disabilities have ". . . higher levels of empathy and altruism, increased tolerance for differences, increased sense of maturity and responsibility, and pride in the sibling's accomplishments."[16]

Professionals' recognition of the strengths and skills required for parenting was sparse during my early years as the mother of a child with a disability. So often the difficulties that I struggled to overcome were taken for granted, and not recognized as an accomplishment to be commended. I would have benefited from hearing more positive encouragement.

Readiness

A model of co-mediation. Although the family has been dealing with this situation for some time and has acquired skills and strengths, these attributes should never be taken for granted. Transitioning is a central event. One of the most crucial periods for families is when the child reaches the age of legal majority, which often coincides with his or her leaving school.[17] Girdner and Earheart suggest a co-mediation model which may assist families at this critical time. They suggest that a skilled counselor and a specialist in the needs of children with disabilities work together with the family to solve problems. In addition to counseling and problem-solving skills, knowledge of human development and family systems is essential for these professionals; and both mediators should be committed to the family's self-determination and control. I would add that they would ideally also be committed to prayer and seeking the Lord's will for the family.

This model has eight steps: initial contact, orientation, definition of the issues, clarification of issues, development of options, establishing preference sets, bargaining, and closure. Each step does not require a separate session.

- The initial contact is self-explanatory.
- In orientation, the process should be thoroughly explained to the family. The family members should be aware that the goal of the sessions is to produce a written document that will reflect their decision regarding the issues at hand. They should also know that the process will occur over a period of time and that everyone's ideas and needs will be considered.
- Definition of issues can occur in conjunction with gathering information from the AFA.
- Clarification of issues will occur as the AFA is considered and all the family members' needs are examined.
- Development of options may take more than one session. The family may need some time between sessions to think about options and talk things over among themselves. This stage should not be rushed. Conflicts may also arise during this phase as family members state their needs or face issues that have been kept down because of the strong emotional content.
- In establishing preference sets, each option will be examined and prioritized. The feasibility of each will be discussed.
- In the bargaining phase, the mediators will facilitate joint decision-making by the couple or the family. This may be the most lively part of the process. The skilled counselor can determine during these exchanges if unresolved issues need attention before honest bargaining can occur. If this is the case, then the process will take considerably longer, and, for a time, the therapist may work with the family with or without the co-mediator to resolve these issues.
- Closure is a finalized, written draft, agreed upon by all. It is not mentioned in the model, but I believe some form of follow-up should exist for the family or parents to check back with the counselor on a periodic basis, perhaps every six months, to determine how the agreements are being kept.[18]

SOME PRACTICAL TIPS

I cannot assume that my own experiences will be applicable to everyone else, but I would like to share some personal observations of what I found helpful as I went through the process of my son moving away from home. As thorough as I tried to be in planning for the event, I learned a lot in the first six months after Chris was in the new living situation that I wished I had known beforehand.

The key, I found, was to ask the right questions. It was not that the staff did not want to give me information—I was just not aware of the proper information to seek to meet my particular needs.

Through trial and error, I found that having the following information *before* my son enrolled would have been very helpful:

- What are the names of all of the staff with whom my son would have any contact?
- What are the specific assignments of each of the staff persons and the days/hours that each person works—specifically, who is day staff, who is night staff, and who is weekend staff?
- Who is the one person who has the most overall contact with and responsibility for Chris?
- What is the best time of day to call that person if needed?
- What is the schedule for work, training, schooling, recreational activities?
- What specific skills would be helpful to my son before entering? For example, I found that training him to recognize his own laundry label would have been very helpful.
- Since his reading was at a very basic level, who will read mail to him?
- What is the best time of day to call my son?
- Can my son call me? Will someone assist him in doing that?
- When are periodic reviews and assessments made of my son's program?
- Can I be a part of that assessment and planning?
- What is the best time of year to enroll? Will the vacations of staff affect my son's orientation and adjustment?
- Ask to see documentation of the residents' human rights.
- Be sure the facility is licensed.
- Inspect all areas, especially living and sleeping areas.
- What is the procedure for laundry and care of clothing?
- Are regular fire drills conducted, and are appropriate safety devices used such as smoke alarms and hot-water temperature regulators?
- What are the policies on home visits?
- What kinds of possessions are advisable to have, such as tape recorders, TVs, or radios? Look at rooms or apartments of others to get an idea of what is feasible.

As transition nears, it would be helpful to begin planning for that next step—perhaps even a year in advance. That may seem like a long time, but the last year of school passes quickly, and it takes some time to prepare for this event both mentally and physically. Keep in mind that no placement for a child will be perfect. No setting can meet all the criteria that parents have in mind as the ideal. That situation does not exist.

If there are conflicts or differences of opinion between parents and staff members, it is essential to think things through and not become overwrought, especially over minor issues, and then to discern the central issues that need action and the items of lesser importance that can be tolerated. It is difficult for a parent to give up care of someone for whom he or she has had primary responsibility for many years.

The day that I was sewing labels on Chris's clothes was particularly distressing for me; I established a pattern of sewing and crying. I was thinking of how only adults in institutions, jails, and the military had labels on their clothes, and of how unjust it was that he could not be treated as non-institutionalized adults are treated. Then, at some point in the day, I began reframing the situation: Chris didn't care whether or not there were labels in his clothes. Kids go away to summer camp with labels in their clothes all the time. This was just a necessary step to get him to the place that was best for him.

Parents experience a wide range of emotions in the placement of a child away from home, and the intensity of emotions deepens with the child's degree of dependence. But preparation can reduce the turmoil. When a parent has made enough of an investigation to feel assured, he or she feels less trauma in turning over care of the child to another. It helps to keep in mind that, while it is not perfect, this is the best situation at this time. Believing this, I have had to trust in God 's provision for my child for right now and for the future.

Parents also need to remember that "magical thinking" can sometimes cloud reality. The family may find that the child who is gone now becomes more desired; memory becomes fuzzy and parents may now be saying that they probably could have managed and should have kept the child at home.

Removing a person from the family system upsets the system, however it may be functioning. The child may have served as a problem focus in the family, and when the child is no longer in the home, other problems that have never been recognized may come to light. Or parents may find that they do not know how to interact with each other and with their other children without the child being present. This is another aspect of the crisis potential for the family when the school bus doesn't come anymore.

CONCLUDING THOUGHTS

Families must face some hard realities when their children with disabilities complete school. In 1986, 67 percent of all Americans with disabilities who were between the ages of sixteen and sixty-four were not working. Of those who were working, 75 percent were employed part time.[19] This shows that mechanisms are not yet in place to ensure effective transitioning of a young adult with disabilities from school to work or to further education. While enrollment in institutions is decreasing, living accommodations in the community have not reciprocally increased, and most young adults with disabilities reside at home, often without vocational and recreational services. Parents receive little support for taking care of these young adults with disabilities at home.

The task of the counselor is complex. Helping families to do what is best for their children with disabilities, as well as for all other members of the family, requires skills in many areas. Use of the AFA and the co-mediation model presented in this chapter may help counselors assist families in resolving some situations in a positive manner.

There are few perfect solutions for helping families in this stage. This is a time when a family's faith is severely tested—a time when faith is proven. With the counselor's guidance, each family will have to work through this transition period in its own way and in its own time. Some passages from Romans 4 and 5 may help the family to gain a perspective on how faith can be their undergirding. In Romans 4:13, we read of how Abraham was not chosen through the law but by faith. Romans 5 describes how we, too, are justified by faith, and because of that faith we have a right to hope. We are then reassured that our hope in God will not disappoint us, because we have all been given the Holy Spirit, by whom God's love is poured into our hearts.

Parents face many uncertainties when trying to plan for their children with disabilities. The tension of trying to live their own lives

while doing what is best for these children becomes a part of their daily lives. The burden of responsibility and care within a context of external constraints beyond their control takes parenting beyond rational and logical bounds. It is only by trusting in God and having supernatural hope that I am able to make any sense at all out of my son's disability. Many parents will attest to feeling this way also.

CHAPTER SEVEN

PROVIDING FOR THE FUTURE

IN 1975 THE NOBEL PRIZE for chemistry was awarded to Sir John W. Cornforth. The fifty-eight-year-old Dr. Cornforth had begun losing his hearing at age fourteen and was totally deaf by age twenty-four. In 1946, the Nobel Prize in chemistry was awarded to James B. Sumner, who lost his left arm in a hunting accident at age seventeen. These two men had to overcome numerous obstacles to succeed, including those who would not support their career goals because of their disabilities.[1]

Every year, in the United States, 250,000 to 300,000 students with disabilities either graduate from high school or complete their allotted years in public education. Relatively few will achieve the levels of success of Cornforth and Sumner. It will be difficult, if not impossible, for many of these young people even to leave home and achieve economic independence. A large percentage of these adult children will be dependent all their lives, to some degree, upon parental support.

EXTENDED PARENTHOOD

Parents of an adult with a developmental disability will not be able to launch that child in a usual fashion because of the dependency of the young person. The amount of parenting required beyond the teen years is directly proportional to the degree of disability of the young adult. The more severe the disabling condition, the greater the dependency, and therefore the increased need to continue acting as a parent. This is particularly true when the disability involves cognitive areas. When the disability involves physical problems only, the young adult may be able to make independent decisions but still depend upon parents or other adults for support in some areas. Young persons with physical impairment are more likely to become independent than will those who have cognitive impairment.

Each situation will be unique. An adult who is blind or deaf, or who has another physical disability may choose to live at home because of economic dependence. As noted in chapter 6, most people with disabilities are unemployed or underemployed, despite their desire and ability to work. It is not always true that parents resist their child's independence, or that the young adult refuses to become independent. Often a child remains dependent because the present system does not support independence for those with disabilities.

Family dysfunction in this situation may be the result of longstanding problems and not a direct result of the young adult's remaining in the home. However, the predicament of the young adult may exacerbate problems already occurring in the family. Either or both parents may have been hoping to experience the empty nest and have more freedom. They may be prohibited from moving either to another geographic area or to a smaller home in their own locality, because of the young adult's disability. They may have to remain where they are either to keep needed services that the locality provides for the young adult, or to provide living space for him or her.

Longevity and Disability

An increasing number of families are facing this kind of extended parenthood. As medical technology improves, many more people with developmental disabilities will have longer life spans. Most of the theory dealing with stress and crisis in the life span is based on stages of the marital couple's lives connected to stages of their children's growth and development. Adequate theory for dealing with adult life stages after children leave is sparse; theory for a marital couple who will have to care for children throughout their lives is virtually nonexistent.

The same medical advances that lengthen the children's life spans also apply to their parents. We are no longer surprised by individuals who are living into their eighties and nineties. Life expectancy in the United States has increased twenty years since 1920.[2] At the same time, the divorce rate has skyrocketed, a trend which should be considered in the context of longevity. Today when we see couples celebrating their fiftieth wedding anniversaries, we are not as surprised by their ages as by the fact that they have remained married that long. If present trends continue, we may be seeing more celebrations of one-hundredth birthdays and fewer fiftieth wedding anniversaries in the future.

Unfortunately, we do not have adequate research or theory to address the problem of aging parents, whether married or single, who are dealing with the adult who has a developmental disability. But this is an issue that will certainly affect these parents and children as they progress in age.

With increased longevity, we have had to revise our concepts of adult development. A parent is more likely now to be involved with a career for a longer period of time. A worker no longer automatically retires at age sixty-five; retirement may be either earlier or later. Both men and women who retire early are likely to have a second or third career.

We need more information and research on the implications of being an "eternal" parent in today's society, and on the effect this responsibility has on career decisions, lifestyles, and quality of life.

ADULT LIFE-SPAN DEVELOPMENT

The average age of the population of the United States is rising steadily. In 1960, 9.2 percent of the population was 65 or over; by the year 2000, that figure will be 13 percent.[3] The concept of adult development has been addressed by many, including Marcus, Neugarten, and Havighurst.[4] However, there is no theory to address aging and being a parent of a dependent adult.

Vivian McCoy presented a realistic view of adult development. She termed adult stages as: ages 35 to 43, mid-life reexamination; 44–55, restabilization; 56–64, preparation for retirement, and 65 +, retirement.[5] McCoy does not discuss involvement with children beyond parental age 55, assuming that by this age, children should be launched. Again, this points to the lack of theory that addresses the issue of the dependent adult child.

Little is written about the transitions in life between these stages. Making a transition implies letting go what is behind and beginning something new. However, a parent of an adult child with a disability finds that the transitions are never complete. The chronic sorrow mentioned in earlier chapters resurfaces from time to time, as new situations are faced. Parents may not feel any personal growth or relief from doubt when challenges arise as replays of earlier struggles, played out on different fields. Never being able to see the child become an independent adult means that a stage of one's life is never completed. As a result, all attempts at personal change must include the element of parenting.

Most of the research on parents of adults with disabilities focuses on adult children who are mentally retarded. Many of these studies discuss programmatic implications. Some issues, however, are relevant to counseling. In one study, mothers of severely disabled young adults were much more likely to suffer from a severe chronic illness and to experience symptoms of psychiatric disturbance than were mothers whose adult children were not disabled. These mothers also had lower participation in the work force and had lower earnings.[6] The severity of the disability was probably a significant factor in this study.

Forty-one families participated in another study of stress. As their institutionalized young adults came home for weekend visits, parental stress levels were related to the demands placed on the parents according to the severity of the disability.[7] Those parents whose children are most capable are apt to experience the least stress and to have the most positive outlook.

Even when the adult is mildly retarded, the parents must still provide extensive support, despite their attempts to foster independence.[8] A study showed that as parents age financial circumstances and unavailability of appropriate caregivers contribute to their unwillingness to leave the adult with other caregivers.[9] An adequate theory about this would also address the phenomenon of women being the primary caregivers in our society and the ones most likely to be affected by having an adult child with a developmental disability. This role usually continues after a divorce, as the mother is most likely to gain custody of and have responsibility for the child with the disability. The increasing numbers of female heads of households, and my own contact with parents supports this conclusion.

A parent's extreme reaction to the stress of caring for a young adult with a disability occurred in Portsmouth, Virginia, where a woman shot her mentally disabled, eighteen-year-old son, and then killed herself. To quote the newspaper report, "His mother's acts were not those of a hateful person, however, neighbors said. Larenda Sivells had tried so hard for so long, and the burden of raising a mentally disabled son who sometimes became angry had become too great, they said."[10]

In a recent study of 228 families where the mothers were at least 55 years of age and had a mentally retarded son or daughter living at home, mothers emerged as the primary caregivers. When both parents were living in the home, the mothers provided personal assistance for the son or daughter 73 percent of the time, and the fathers 37 percent of the time. Fathers helped more with minor home repairs, and mothers and fathers participated equally in motility (helping with movement, such as up and down stairs) and transportation.[11] Even though the figure of 37 percent seems low, older fathers' involvement in care was higher than that of fathers of young children with developmental disabilities, who participate far less in childcare activities.[12]

The problem is more complicated when the middle-aged parents of a child with a disability also have aging or elderly parents with needs. Particularly if he or she is single, a parent who must deal with problems of aging parents and of an adult child with a disability is a candidate for emotional and/or physical distress. These stresses will differ according to the residential arrangements of all parties involved. But even when the parent resides alone, if he or she has financial or decision-making responsibilities for the parents and the adult child, stressors and pressures are inevitable.

A MODEL FOR EXTENDED PARENTING

We cannot accurately predict what will occur in a family as the child with the disability progresses through adulthood, because all families differ in their circumstances. However, we can describe common stages families will experience as the young adult with the disability leaves school and begins adult life.

Transitioning

The first stage is the transitioning period immediately after high school. This was discussed in detail in the previous chapter. Whether the young adult is residing in the home or elsewhere, this stage will include a period of adjustment that can last from a few months to over a year. The greater the changes and the more complex the necessary accommodations, the longer the family members need to progress through transition. Residential and vocational issues also will be a part of this period.

Adaptation

The next stage will be reached once transition has occurred. A new rhythm of life is established, and the parents begin thinking of how they will live out the future with this new circumstance. Meanwhile, other children may be graduating from high school or college, marrying, moving out of the home, and getting on with their lives.

If they have not done so previously, parents at this stage may become aware of the need to provide for their child's future. They also must face their own mortality and make plans to care for the adult child when they will no longer be able to meet his or her needs, either because they are incapacitated or have died.

Adaptation of the family will differ, depending upon whether or not other children are still in the home, and whether or not the adult with the disability lives there.

If other children in the family have left, a new stage occurs. If the adult with a disability has remained in the home, there will be no empty nest; the couple will become a permanent triad. Vacations, meals out, recreation, and leisure will be a matter of three people, not two.

If the adult with a disability is living away from home, the couple experiences being alone, and interaction and contact with the adult child is most likely to be on a limited basis, perhaps fitting into their lives at their convenience. This freedom will be a new experience to the couple, one which may bring either great delight in being together or crisis because they have grown so far apart that they do not know how to interact with each other without the child.

No matter what situation exists, any one of several events can occur that might precipitate a crisis: death or incapacitation of a parent, financial problems, loss of a job, or divorce. While these events can bring about a crisis in any family, the adult with a disability is more likely to feel the direct effects than any other sibling. To the person with a disability, the event can represent the loss of a caregiver, an advocate, financial support, and of a personal loving relationship. When one parent dies or becomes incapacitated, the remaining parent may not be able to continue the burden of care. While other siblings are able to compensate for these losses in their own lives, the adult with the disability is less likely to be able to replace these essential components to the same degree.

As their ability to meet the needs of the adult child decreases, parents will have to face increased interaction with and dependence upon outside service providers. As a result, they may experience the same stress they felt in dealing with professionals in earlier years. This time, however, the stress may be increased because the options may appear more limited as parents' own personal resources decrease. A sense of loss of control and futility may result, especially if parents feel that their adult child is in a less-than-optimal situation and they are powerless to change it.

Strategies for Future Planning

The remaining sections of this chapter will deal with practical considerations for the family, as categorized in "Readiness," the last section of the Five-Factor Model. In these circumstances, failing to prepare is truly preparing to fail. Only by making definite plans can parents ensure that the child's future welfare is carried out according to their wishes.

There are a number of items parents should consider in making these plans. First, parents should develop a long-range plan for the adult child's life which could be continued after their deaths. For parents of young children, many items will be uncertain; but they will become more relevant over time. Parents should review both their plans and their wills about every five years to keep up with changes in the child's growth, development, needs, and family situations.

In making plans, parents should ask, "What kind of a life do I want for this person?" That question is linked to a realistic assessment of abilities, capabilities, needs, and desires of the child, and of available resources.

The global question can be answered by an appraisal of specific areas in the child's life—the living situation, vocational interests, recreational and leisure pursuits, church support, personal needs and interests, and legal considerations.

Establishing a Trust

The provisions each family makes will be linked to their own financial circumstances. A relatively new and innovative method that is growing in popularity is the use of a trust, which can provide future finances and guardianship for the person with a disability. This is not the customary trust set up in conjunction with a bank; it is a new concept.

The November 1988 issue of *Money* magazine devoted several pages to this kind of plan made by the Banning family. The Bannings' son, Steve, who was nineteen when the article was written, is disabled due to an injury that occurred when he was eight. The Bannings founded PLAN (Planned Lifetime Assistance Network), a trust to provide services and general living needs from parents' estates to those with disabilities. In 1988 eighty families were part of PLAN.[13] Several separate trusts now operate throughout the United States to provide financial and personal assistance for individuals with disabilities after their parents die. Some are statewide trusts; others are community based. A list of some of these trusts is provided in Appendix III.

These are generally revocable trusts while the grantor is alive, but become irrevocable after his or her death. A trust is not just for wealthy parents; it can be funded by an insurance policy, requiring no large investment by parents. The trust document can provide guardianship, details of where the adult child will live, and types of treatment desired; in other words, parents can use this document to provide a clear guide of their wishes for their child after their deaths. Trusts are administered in a variety of ways; but generally there is a board of individuals to make decisions and monitor care of the adult child. If parents do not live in a state or province that has such a trust, they may be interested in starting one, as the Bannings did.

As difficult as pondering the reality of one's death may be, parental decisions must be made for the welfare of the adult child with a disability. If parents do not make their wishes known in a manner consistent with the law, they are giving the state the power to make these crucial decisions for them, and putting the future of their child into the hands of the government.

Family Participation in Planning

When planning does occur, all family members, including the person with a disability, should participate as much as possible. It is a misperception that those who are considered as moderately or mildly retarded have little or no perception of their disabilities.[14] The adult child has a preference for environment, work, and leisure, as well as some awareness of his or her limitations. So this child's autonomy should be considered. The ideal is that as much as his or her capabilities allow, the person with the disability should have a voice in choosing the future.

Children who do not have disabilities should also have both information and input in choosing their guardians in the event of both parents' death. Young parents do not often think of the possibility of their own demise; if they do, they may think that grandparents would be the natural persons to assume care of the children. This may not always be the best course of action, however, particularly if the child has a disability.

Regardless of what specific plans are made, all parents should make a will when the first child is born. Mothers and fathers should have separate wills, and guardianships should be specifically noted.

Sibling Responsibilities

Parents may assume that siblings will eventually take over the responsibilities for the person with a disability. But that may or may not be feasible for several reasons. The problem is not that siblings are not caring or loving individuals. However, in today's transient society, brothers and sisters are likely to have moved away from home, perhaps to another state. They may not know the adult child as a person and will not be aware of his or her likes, dislikes, needs, and desires. If the adult child has been living outside the family home, the siblings may never have visited that residence. They may not know the system or the care providers in the residential placement or in the community. Suddenly having to care for or to find placement for an adult with a disability could throw their lives into chaos.

For all these reasons, parents have an obligation to provide a road map for the well-being of both the person with a disability and of his or her siblings. They should provide for the future of the person with a disability without putting undue pressure on the other family members. A sibling should not have to choose a marriage partner based on whether or not that person would be willing to have the brother or sister with a disability live with them someday.[15]

Residential Planning

Living situations encompass a wide range of possibilities for the adult child, and each family will have to make individual determinations of what is best for them and their child. The following list addresses situations of the adult child living outside the family home or the home of other relatives, progressing from least restrictive to most restrictive:

1. The person may be *completely independent* as any other person would be, living alone or with a roommate, or being either single or married. Some developmental disabilities have little or no effect on the person's ability to function. These are most likely to be congenital disorders of a physical nature, such as a cleft palate.
2. The person may live in relative independence, alone or with roommates, needing only *occasional monitoring* of financial matters and perhaps some occasional financial assistance.
3. The person may live alone or with others, but require someone to *monitor weekly* his or her need for assistance with daily life (household chores and cooking, grocery and personal shopping, financial management, and personal care, such as getting regular haircuts).
4. The person may live alone or with roommates and require *daily help* with cooking, shopping, monitoring of personal care, and household chores.
5. The residence may be one in which someone is always present to function as a *houseparent,* with the business of life occurring as it does in any household.
6. Because of needs for safety of self and others, the person may require a residence where there is a *night staff that stays awake,* as opposed to the previous situation, in which the houseparents sleep at night.
7. The most restrictive environment is *twenty-four-hour supervisory and medical care,* which some persons may require.

Parents must also bear in mind the importance of the location of the adult child's residence because the location determines which other community services will he provided. The distance of the residence from other family members and the ease of paying visits to the adult child, or of his or her ability to visit others is an additional concern.

Some Specialized Situations

When the adult child has a cognitive impairment, he or she needs security, safety, and comfortable surroundings in an atmosphere of nurturance. So future planning for his or her residential placement is critical. Surely all parents would like to guarantee that their children will live with people who will be kind, caring, and professional. Christian parents may want their adult child to live in a setting of Christian love and values.

A residential facility's philosophy toward those with disabilities is a key factor in determining programming and services. Some facilities may view their roles as custodial and paternalistic; their main purpose is to keep adults protected and isolated. Others may see their function as providing as normal an environment as possible, with almost laissez-faire management.

The majority of adults with disabilities who live in residences outside of family homes are in facilities which receive staffing and services from public or private nonprofit organizations. Their philosophical foundations are likely to be secular, with little regard for clients' spirituality. Some residences are run by Christian organizations; but the concept of what Christian means varies widely and is idiosyncratic to each facility.

Christian parents will have a natural concern with the values and philosophy of those who care for their adult children. They may also be concerned that the faith imparted by the parents is continued through prayer, Christian fellowship, Bible reading, and Sunday services.

Most communities have group homes, residential schools, and larger institutions; those with disabilities are designated as "clients," others are "staff."

Another residential concept for people with disabilities is community life. Communities are not as well known as group homes, residential schools, or larger institutions because they require a commitment and philosophy that is very different from the client-staff model used in those facilities. Two such international communities are L'Arche and Camphill Villages.

L'Arche (the ark) is an international federation of homes for people with mental disabilities. Jean Vanier began the L'Arche communities in France in 1964 when he took two men into his own home in Trosly. There are now homes in seventeen countries, including twenty-three homes in Canada and eleven in the United States. (See Appendix IV.) Each L'Arche home operates in the concept of Christian community.

The homes minister to those with disabilities, as well as to the assistants who voluntarily come to live there for varying lengths of stay, whether a year, or five years, or a lifetime.

Christianity is not a requirement for these volunteer assistants. But to read any of Vanier's books is to discover a deep Christian spirituality which is reflected in L'Arche homes. Vanier's devotion to those with disabilities comes from his love of and relationship with Christ. In his book, *Community and Growth*, he wrote, "I began L'Arche in 1964, in the desire to live the Gospel and to follow Jesus Christ more closely. Each day brings me new lessons on how much Christian life must grow in commitment to life in community, and on how much that life needs faith, the love of Jesus and the presence of the Holy Spirit if it is to deepen."[16] A directory of L'Arche homes is included in Appendix IV. A listing of Vanier's books is in Appendix II.

Another federation of communities is the Camphill Villages, based on Rudolf Steiner's concept of arthroposophy, a path to understanding humans in their relationship with the physical and spiritual world. Camphill was begun in 1939 by Dr. Karl Koenig, who established a therapeutic community in Scotland for refugee children with special needs. The village concept was created as the children became adults.

Today there are over sixty Camphill communities around the world, with six in the United States (five villages and one village school) and one in Ontario.

Camphill Villages recognize that in each individual there is an intact, inviolable spiritual integrity. They profess a nondenominational, Christian way of life, holding Bible studies and Sunday services, and celebrating the passing of seasons and holidays. The villages have different activities, ranging from agriculture to crafts such as candlemaking and weaving.[17] As in L'Arche, nondisabled people live with residents and participate in the community life. Appendix IV also lists a directory of Camphill Villages.

VOCATIONAL PLANNING

Vocational Interests

The vocational interests of a person with disabilities cannot be totally separated from the living situation. Often, the person's work opportunities are linked directly to where he or she resides. Although a compromise of accepting a less-than-optimal work situation may be necessary to obtain the desired residence, the interests and abilities of the person should be matched with the work situation as closely as possible. This work is important because it is more than something to do in exchange for pay. It is also a source of social identity and happiness; and it prevents boredom, and contributes to self-esteem. These factors are as crucial to persons with disabilities as they are to anyone else.

However, for most, opportunity for work is limited. So it is crucial to first determine which situation is most likely to be appropriate for that person, and then try to match his or her interests to work within that setting.

Hierarchy of Work Placements

The following work placements proceed from least restrictive to most restrictive, or from those requiring the highest level of independence to those requiring the least.

1. The person is able to both obtain a job independently and live on wages received.
2. A person requires a job coach or trainer to work with him or her on the job for a time to teach the specific skills; then the person can work with only the same kind of supervision any other person on that job would require.
3. The person is able to work singly or in a crew, or job enclave, with a special trainer or supervisor always on the site.
4. The person can work only in a sheltered workshop setting. The pay received in these circumstances may be minimal.
5. The person cannot do any type of work at all, and requires a daytime activity that is appropriate for his or her capabilities.

In general, persons in group homes or independent/assisted-living apartments have jobs or attend daytime activities. In larger residential facilities, residents may work on site or in a community job, or attend daily activities. At L'Arche, residents who are able work out in the local community; or at large homes such as Daybreak in Toronto, they work within the residential community. At Camphill Villages, residents generally work in the villages.

RECREATION AND LEISURE

Play is the life work of the child. To adults, recreational or leisure pursuits are secondary to work, but they continue to be an important part of life. This is no less true for a person with a disability. But all too often, his or her recreation takes on a single dimension—watching TV. For adults with disabilities, recreation and leisure are crucial, because too often, social isolation accompanies the disability. Many of these adults do not have the ability to plan for their own leisure pursuits. Or if they can choose activities, they may lack the companionship, transportation, or resources to enjoy them.

In one study, half of the surveyed adolescents with spina bifada reported not visiting with or going out with a friend in the previous twelve months. Social isolation tended to be higher for those in special schools than it was for those in regular schools.[18] For those who are not residing with family members, the isolation may be more poignant, with their social groups limited to others with disabilities— and staff members.

Parents should inquire as to how leisure and recreational activities will be provided for their child in a residential setting. Will there be sports, participation in Special Olympics, dances, or attendances at plays, concerts, and movies? Does the local recreation department offer therapeutic recreation facilities and programs? Will there be provision for an annual vacation?

Examples of widely varied activities are provided by Ocean House, a Virginia Beach residence which is used by local families from September to April for respite care, and is open during the summer months for week-long vacations for persons with disabilities. Ocean House is located a few steps from the beach and its activities include trips to nearby tourist attractions. Other programs provide tours specifically organized for people with disabilities to go to Disneyworld and other places.

Many summer camps are specifically designed for adults with disabilities. And L'Arche homes residents often travel to other countries.[19]

Another consideration in residential planning is the adult child's preference for certain possessions that are important to him or her. The residential setting should allow the person to have those possessions available for use and be safe from theft or damage by others. Julie, for example, loves music, and her parents want her to have access to her tapeplayer and tapes. Andrew loves baseball cards and enjoys having others come and view his collection. Dale collects comic books and enjoys reading his favorites. All of these persons should have access to those things that give them pleasure; we all need enrichment in our lives. A residential setting that does not allow for these personal pursuits would be delivering a reduced quality of life.

Church Attendance

Church attendance also should be considered in planning The church can be a place of contact with the larger society as well as a source of spiritual enrichment. Chapter 10, which deals with the role of the church, discusses this aspect in more detail.

Continuing Education

We adults do not stop all learning at age twenty-one. Nor do people with disabilities. Education is a lifelong endeavor and should be kept in mind when parents are planning their child's future. Educational programs for persons with disabilities range from formal courses at the community college level to practical-living courses that may be offered through local colleges or community services. Some residential facilities may have formal, daily schooling and combine traditional school subjects with independent living skills, such as cooking or grocery shopping.

Financial Planning

Life Insurance

In most families, the father has life insurance to provide for his family if he dies. However, the mother often is not insured, particularly if she does not work outside of the home. But when there is a child with a disability, the cost of replacing the services (and wages, if applicable) of the mother should be considered, and sufficient insurance should be carried on her life. Also, both parents should have some type of disability insurance to cover their becoming disabled by disease or accident. Ideally, this insurance covers lost wages and care for the child.

Awareness of Restrictions of SSI

Most persons with developmental disabilities will receive SSI, beginning either as a child or after attaining age eighteen. Very strict limits govern the amount of money a person can have in assets or income, either earned or unearned, while receiving SSI. In light of these limits, parents must be aware of the consequences of their child inheriting property or money from either their estate or the estate of other relatives, unless the amounts involved are so great that there is no need for the person with a disability to collect any SSI.

Because of these restrictive laws, the trust is once again a practical option for persons with disabilities. Money in the trust can provide for needs and extras without jeopardizing SSI, which, by itself, only provides a living below the poverty level.

Parents also should determine any limits on pension funds that would be given to the adult child. Few military people seem to be aware that military survivors benefits can be designated to the child who is disabled. Military personnel can, at retirement, ensure an income to their child for life at little cost.

The Parental Will

Two people will be crucial to the future of the adult child after the death of his or her parents. The first is the lawyer chosen to draft the parents' wills. This lawyer should have some knowledge of the regulations that affect persons with disabilities. And if a community trust is available, the lawyer should know how to incorporate the trust into the wills. Parents should interview lawyers about their expertise in these matters before engaging them to perform this important job. If the parents cannot obtain a satisfactory person on their own, the local disability-related organizations may be able to provide referrals.

The second crucial person is the one who is appointed legal guardian. This may or may not be the person who will have guardianship of the other children. It may be a sibling who is of legal age. Whether the guardian is a relative or a friend, he or she should be able to be an advocate, willing to learn the system and to deal with others for the welfare of the person. The guardian should not be content to leave all decisions up to agency or residential staff.

SEXUALITY

The usual area of concern that few people want to address is the sexuality of this adult child. We're all sexual beings from birth, and this includes the person with a disability. Often, we may think of these persons with disabilities as eternal children. But they are not. They are adults with adult desires and needs that may differ in degree from most other adults; but still they must be considered as adults.

The trend of normalization begun in the 1960s is continuing, with the expectation that those with disabilities will be participating in the community as much as possible.[20] Those whose IQs range from fifty-five to eighty-five may have been labeled as moderately or mildly retarded in school; but once they leave school, they are not likely to be labeled any longer. They can usually work, and perhaps no one will challenge their right to marry and have children.[21]

Parents can begin to be aware of their children's needs for sexual education while they are in school and in the home, and to prepare them for what they will need as adults. Abramson, Parker and Weisberg point out some significant results found in several studies. For example, many parents do not recognize that their children have sexual needs, nor do they wish their children to receive sex education, because they fear they will become overstimulated and preoccupied with sex. Problems arise primarily with issues of pregnancy, homosexuality, and masturbation. Courts have decided against sterilization and prohibition of sexual experience by those with mental retardation; so it would seem that education and training would be the logical next step. But these are measures that both parents and staff seem reluctant to pursue.[22]

In addition, we know that those who have disabilities are at high risk for physical and sexual abuse. This risk might be lessened if the young adult has enough information to protect herself or himself against such abuse. This information should be appropriate to the person's level of understanding, and explained in terms that he or she can comprehend.

Masturbation also seems to be a topic of difficulty for parents, and may be clouded by moral teachings received when they were young. Those who have disabilities are sexual beings and require some outlet for sexual expression. This is not to say that parents should undertake to teach their children the mechanics of masturbation. However, when a young adult chooses this activity, parents can provide some guidelines, such as using the bedroom or bathroom, not touching genitals in public, not coercing others into sexual activity, and not allowing others to coerce them. I realize this topic may be considered controversial by some people. My intention here is only to offer some general comments which others may or may not find valid.

Jean Vanier discusses masturbation and other aspects of sexuality for those with disabilities in *Man and Woman He Made Them*. His emphasis is on the need for love, and the wholeness and completeness of the person.

My experience shows that the sexual drive is more often a cry for relationship than a cry for pleasure. Often it erupts when someone feels alone and anguished. It then seeks expression on the level of genital sexuality. . . . Many people with a mental handicap do not believe either in the beauty of their person or in their capacity to love profoundly and to be loved. . . . The goal of education is to help people grow toward wholeness and to discover their place, and eventually exercise their gifts, in a network of friendship, and, ideally, in an acknowledged covenant relationship. This means the integration of one's sexuality in a vision of fellowship and friendship."[23]

Socially Appropriate Behavior

Learning socially appropriate behavior is another part of protecting oneself from sexual abuse. Many children with disabilities receive and give a lot of hugs in school, in the family, and in church, and these are fine and appropriate. However, as a person's world expands, he or she must distinguish between touching significant people and friends, and touching strangers; boundaries should also be set to establish who may or may not touch the person. Parents should inquire into the kinds of social activities, dating, and heterosexual activities encouraged or permitted in a residential facility. Also, parents will want to know the facility's policy on permitting or discouraging homosexual relationships.

CUTTING THE UMBILICAL CORD

Professionals may view parents as overprotective when they try to make all of these arrangements and specify, as much as possible, their desires for the child. But according to author Carol Tingey, overprotection is a myth perpetrated by professionals. There is valid concern for protection of the adult child's physical and mental well-being. The reason that some parents cannot "cut the umbilical cord," says Tingey, is that "the world is not yet a suitable place for their child."[24] Parents need to do as much as they can to protect and provide for the adult child when they are living. They must also provide for the child's needs when they are no longer living, because, at that time, the umbilical cord will indeed be irrevocably cut. Then it will be only their preparation that will enable their adult child to live in the situation they desire.

CHAPTER EIGHT

EFFECTS ON THE MARITAL COUPLE
AND THE SIBLINGS

A FAMILY IS A SYSTEM that is greater than the sum of its individual parts. When a family has a child with a disability, the effects are felt both by the family as a whole and by each family member. Yet each member's individual reaction will be, in some way, tempered by the fact that he or she is part of this particular family. The unique dynamics of each particular family which has a child with a disability must be considered during counseling.

PROBLEMS WITH PAST RESEARCH

Past research is of little practical value to the counselor in helping the family of a child with a disability. To have such a child is not a pathological condition, so the counselor cannot refer to a diagnostic manual to verify patterns of behavior. And the literature on stressors experienced by these families is inconclusive.[1] Researchers also disagree when reporting the divorce rate of these families. Some place it at nine times as high as the general population, while others estimate it at three times or one and a half times as high.[2] Still other researchers say it is comparable to that of the general population.[3]

The counselor looking for a methodology to deal with families will not welcome the fact that ". . . there is no singular statement one could make regarding the impact of a handicapped child on the psychological well-being of his or her parents . . . there is no normative data available on families of handicapped children. Consequently, it is impossible to identify ranges of psychological health and dysfunction for such families."[4]

CHARACTERISTICS OF A HEALTHY FAMILY

Rather than report on studies that are limited in their application, I have chosen instead to focus on the characteristics of a healthy family. Within that framework we can investigate possible barriers to healthy functioning in a family that has a child with a disability. With this picture of health in mind, the counselor can then assist the family to target areas in which it can improve.

The family's demographic details can be gathered through use of the AFA. Then the counselor can then begin to explore those areas that will impact on the family's ability to develop and maintain healthy characteristics.

Florence Kaslow has developed a list of eight characteristics of healthy families that indicate optimal functioning. The term *optimal* was chosen rather than *normal* because normal is considered to be only mid-range functioning, somewhere between healthy and dysfunctional.[5] (See Figure 8–1)

The Range of Family Functioning

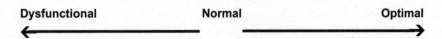

Dysfunctional **Normal** **Optimal**

Figure 8–1

A Sense of the Family as a System

The first characteristic of a healthy family is that the family has a sense of itself as a system where all members have a very special relationship with one another. They realize that the family is greater than the sum of the individual members. The parents have a strong sense of fidelity and total commitment to one another, providing a stable environment. The family is also responsive to outside input, expectations, and challenges.

Family Boundaries. The family also has clear generational boundaries; for most families, that would be the parental and child(ren) boundaries. There are also semi-permeable boundaries between the family and the environment in which it exists. In contrast, the family of a child with a disability can become remote and isolated.[6] Family members may not access help; or when they do, they do so in a belligerent manner. This can occur when parents become worn down by the constant need to interact with these outside systems, and as a result choose to close themselves off.

In some situations, one parent refuses to interact, leaving the other spouse to make most or all outside contacts regarding the child. For example, Charlotte was the one who attended all the parent meetings with her daughter Barbara's teachers; her husband Harry did not want to get involved with school matters. When a parent support group was formed at the school, Charlotte asked Harry to attend with her. He would not, and she went alone. Within this group, Barbara learned to share her feelings with other parents of children with disabilities, and she was helped by this interaction. As Harry saw her becoming calmer and able to make better decisions about Barbara, he started to express his frustrations and feelings. He expected her to tell him each week what she had learned in the group, but he was not interested in reading the material or in changing his actions.

In reality, he wanted to use Charlotte to dump his feelings on, while continuing on with his same behaviors, including increased time spent at work to be away from the pressures of dealing with Barbara's needs. Family conflict occurred as Harry saw Charlotte as the family member who crossed the family boundary into the community to bring back input. Charlotte, on the other hand, felt that the family as a whole needed a more permeable boundary with the outside supporting environment.

Recognition of Growth and Change. A healthy system recognizes growth and change as normal. But in the family of a child with a disability, change may be viewed as another burden because so much energy is required to accommodate it. The key points mentioned in earlier chapters (diagnosis, entering school, puberty, and leaving school) are all times when the family members must adapt and adjust. And they must remain flexible to deal with the developmental schedule of the child with the disability, which will not be like that of the other children.

Sharing of Roles and Chores. Members of the healthy system share roles and chores. In contrast, when there is a child with a disability, one family member may be seen as the principal caretaker. Usually, this is the mother; or, if this role is assigned to a child, it is usually the oldest daughter. For all in the family to shift in their roles and share the caretaking responsibilities requires abandoning traditional perceptions. Often the fear of changing these roles keeps people frozen in old ways of functioning that existed before the child with the disability was born.

For example, Bob grew up in a household where the roles of his parents were strictly defined: His mother cared for the house and the children, and his father worked outside the home. His father's interaction with the three children was primarily that of disciplinarian and financial provider. Bob and his wife Marie had two children, and the oldest, David, twelve, was developmentally delayed and continued to wet the bed. Both Bob and Marie worked; but Bob refused to change David's sheets in the morning and put them into the washer. He viewed that chore as part of the laundry, which was strictly Marie's domain. Bob and Marie would benefit from being able to discuss role definition within their household.

While other family members may *choose* not to change their roles, the child who has a disability often *cannot* take on new roles. His or her ability to share in the household work may be limited, or only done with constant supervision. In this situation, one of three problems may develop. First, the parents may begin to treat all the children as more dependent than they really are, with rules that are inappropriate for their ages and requiring a more highly structured environment. Second, the child with the disability may face the constant frustration of failing to meet inflexible, child-role expectations. Third, the parents may set a double standard which can create hard feelings in the siblings.

Generational Boundaries

Healthy families have clearly distinct boundaries between each generation of parents, grandparents, and children. On the other hand, the family of a child with a disability may not have these clear distinctions of generational boundaries. For example, it may be difficult for these parents to maintain their need for privacy as a couple, particularly if their child requires intense medical attention, or if the child only sleeps a few hours at a time. The logistical problems of baby-sitting may make it difficult for this couple to spend evenings out or to take a weekend alone as needed.

It is also possible that other children in this family may cross the boundary into the parental domain as the siblings care for the child.

Blurring of Parental Boundaries. Parents of a newborn often find that their private relationship has taken second place to the helpless baby who manages to dominate their lives. To some degree, the parents of a child with a disability face this prospect for all of their lives.

Over time, each parent will define his or her relationship with this child. A parent may become strongly identified with the child with the disability. If this occurs, there will be a direct relationship between the degree of disability and the intensity of the bonding—which may result in the deterioration of the parental couple's private relationship. The opposite could also occur, with one or both of the parents rejecting the child, causing bonding to fail to occur. If there is a divergence, with one parent identifying strongly with the child and the other emotionally dissociating, the relationship of the couple is in even greater jeopardy.

If one parent becomes the primary caregiver to the child with a disability, there is a danger that he or she may become self-identified as only being a caregiver. If the caregiver is the mother, the result may be a lack of opportunity to develop her own interests and meet her own needs. She may extend "super caregiving" to all members of the family, especially if the father is a minimal caregiver. In this role, she may not allow them to function for themselves, but expend her energies to meet everyone else's needs. By doing so, she relieves others of the responsibility to participate in the family.

Grandparents. The generational boundaries involving grandparents may not fit classic systems definitions in the family of a child with a disability. The grandparents in this family may be needed for physical help and/or financial support; and in a sense, they may become another set of parents. While some might say that such a situation of co-parenting by parents and grandparents is an unhealthy one, it may be a necessary part of the family's support system for a time. In fact, in many cultures, cross-generational shared parenting is a healthy and accepted norm. In comparison, grandparent-grandchild relationships in the United States have been neglected in counseling situations. This is unfortunate, as they could prove to be significant relationships for all children, whether disabled or not.[7] Each situation will be different; but each family should be allowed to define what works for them at this particular time. In some instances, the grand-parents' participation may actually free the parents to maintain their boundaries from their children.

Marge and Phil, for example, are able to take occasional weekends away and an annual vacation alone as a couple because Marge's parents are willing to care for their two children, including ten-year-old Susan, who cannot be left alone because she often has seizures. The grandparents' temporary roles as caregivers are simplified by the single notebook in which Marge keeps schedules and medication instructions for Susan and a list of phone numbers for the doctor, the school, and neighbors who could be contacted in case of emergency. She only has to update this one book when they are planning a trip. Marge and Phil still cannot just spontaneously decide to go away. They must plan in advance and coordinate schedules with Marge's parents; but it is worth the effort to be able to get away.

Clear Communication

A healthy family has clear channels of communication. This communication includes consistency between verbal and nonverbal messages.

Openness. A healthy family functions in a setting of openness that allows conflicts to be resolved. Members are free to disagree, to express their opinions, or to ask for clarification.

Within this kind of open environment, Jan and Adam told fifteen-year-old Josh that their family, including five-year-old Mark, who is developmentally delayed, would all be going on a vacation in July to Adam's parents. Josh, who had hopes of getting a summer job, was able to ask his parents about specific dates and what this would mean to his job plans without his parents becoming defensive and accusing him of thinking only for himself. He could express his concerns about the job, and also about his responsibilities for Mark during vacation without his parents verbally attacking him for asking questions.

Another facet of openness in communication revolves around the nature of the child's disability. A healthy family will disclose all aspects regarding the child, giving siblings all the information they are able to handle for their ages. In a healthy family, members are also allowed to express their feelings regarding the disability. For example, Jill is allowed to tell her parents that she feels uncomfortable when they are pushing her sister, Jana, in her wheelchair around the shopping mall because of how other people look at them. Jill's mother, Nancy, uses the opportunity to discuss how other people do not quite know what to do or say about people with disabilities. Nancy and Jill can also think of ways to lessen her discomfort, and also weigh the costs of feeling uncomfortable against the pleasure they give Jana by taking her out.

Many problems of siblings revolve around others' reactions to the child with a disability. With clear communication, the family can discuss how to answer other children's unkind remarks. If the solution to the family's problems with outsiders is to keep the child with a disability in the house and always get baby-sitters when they go on outings, then trouble exists in that family.

Because of the physical needs involved, planning for outings is more complex for the family when there is a child with a disability. And the more complex the task, the more clarity in communication is required.

Directness. Clear communication also involves giving direct messages. One parent should not make remarks to a child in the hope that the child will in turn convey the message to the other parent. When this occurs, an intra-family boundary is violated and a child is drawn in an unhealthy fashion into the parental system.

This is the situation in Diane's family. As wife and mother she has cared for the children, but now she is becoming resentful when her husband, Mike, goes on frequent hunting trips and leaves her alone with them. She would also like to have some time to herself, but does not know how to ask for it. Instead, she says to Patty, age twelve, "Isn't it awful how Dad always leaves us at home with Danny [age nine and visually impaired] while he and his buddies are off having a good time?"

When other family problems are present, the following scene might occur if Diane decides to express her feelings:

Diane: When you go off hunting so often and leave me alone, I feel left with all of the responsibility.

Mike: The kids are big enough to take care of themselves. What kind of big deal is it? You always criticize what I do

Diane: It is a big deal to me. I would occasionally like some opportunities for weekends, or even a day of a weekend, to myself.

Mike: Well, when deer hunting is over, it's fishing season. If you want to arrange for someone else to watch the kids, you go ahead and do what you want.

Mike recognizes none of Diane's feelings and if he will not discuss these issues, then Diane has to decide that if she has to get away, she either will have to make the childcare arrangements herself, or announce her plans in advance of Mike's so he would have to make them. Either situation is not one that promotes open communication and intimacy in the couple. But by taking action, Diane may force some of these issues to come to light.

If, however, there are some strengths in the marriage, the scene might proceed differently:

Diane: When you go off hunting so often and leave me alone, I feel left with all of the responsibility.

Mike: I wasn't aware of how you felt; I just thought you could handle things as you always do.

Diane: I can handle things, but I would like an opportunity to have an occasional weekend alone also, or to spend a Saturday with my friends.

Mike: I'm sorry, Diane, I didn't realize I was being so selfish. I don't want to have to give up hunting and fishing altogether, though. What did you have in mind?

From this point, Mike and Diane can work out a solution that allows both of them leisure time within a framework of shared childcare responsibility. They may even proceed to carve out some time alone together as a couple.

Power in the Marital Dyad

A healthy family has an equality of power between the marital pair. And while the marital coalition is strong, it also is flexible. This couple's decision making is based on mutuality, with information shared and consensus reached, even though it is likely that one partner has more expertise in some areas than the other. Not all decisions have to be by consensus, however; either partner may make the decision after prior consultation with the other.

Decision-making. In comparison with this ideal situation, one marital partner may decide to dump all duties of decision-making about the child with a disability on the other spouse. Or one spouse may decide to make decisions about the child or family matters and not inform the other. Either situation is especially dangerous if the withdrawn partner then becomes critical of decisions reached.

Financial power may be a component in decision-making when the spouse who is working outside the home or the one with the larger paycheck makes singular decisions. Parents set the stage for this situation if they define responsibilities for the household and the children as one person's domain and financial decisions as the role of the other. If the couple lacks open communication, then unilateral, secret decisions may be made. If either partner lacks a commitment to fidelity, then singular, secret decision-making may become a pattern.

Shared Leadership. Children should be aware of a mutually submissive, shared leadership style in the executive branch of the family. With shared leadership, children can take on some adult responsibilities and privileges without violating the family's internal generational boundaries. In this environment, the "Archie Bunker chair" reserved for Dad only, the rigid rules about who sits where at dinner, or set expectations about who always does what to prepare the evening meal are less likely to exist.

In contrast, when parents do not share leadership in the family, they are less likely to allow input from the siblings regarding the child with a disability. And they are less likely to have communication channels that allow expression of feelings. The siblings may then feel less of a connection to that child because of being shut out.

Encouragement of Independence in Children

In a healthy family, the parents foster autonomy and independence in children, preparing them for the day when they can leave the family. Previous chapters on transitioning and planning for the child's future discussed some possible conflicts in this area when a child with a disability is involved. These parents may desire to foster autonomy but be unable to do so because the appropriate support services for those with disabilities are lacking.

Dependence in the Child with a Disability. It is unhealthy when the parents, to meet their own needs, keep the child with a disability dependent. They may not even consider independence for the child because he or she is the only thing that keeps their relationship going. And even when that relationship is not ideal, they may be resistant to any changes in it. For example, they may be triangulated with the child and not know how to function without him or her as the center of their existence. Triangulation is a concept in family systems theory that explains what occurs when two people from separate generational systems align together to the exclusion of, or against, a third family member. When one parent becomes triangulated with the child, it takes the pressure off of him or her to have a real relationship with the other spouse.

Dependence of Siblings. Parents may not encourage the independence of their other children, either, because they have come to depend on the care and companionship the siblings provide the child with a disability. To have the other children become independent and move away would threaten the support system which has cared for the needy child. But if the parents are open to alternatives for the one with the disability, there is no crisis situation.

Parental Modeling of Healthy Emotions

In healthy families, parents model appropriate emotions, with a wide range being the norm. On the other hand, a family caring for a child with a disability can become so overburdened that good times are not allowed. The father may retreat into workaholism, modeling the idea that having fun as a family is not a priority.

At the other extreme, the parents may be so concerned with keeping up the family spirits that they never allow the children to see them feeling their grief about the situation. A family meeting to discuss issues of how people are feeling may allow a full range of emotional expressions, as well as an opportunity to discuss role flexibility.

A Sense of Humor. A healthy family is optimistic and has a sense of humor. This humor is shared, appropriate, and not aimed at one member. My son Chris loves to sit in front of the TV with a tray of peanuts, then shell and eat them as he watches his favorite shows. He carefully dumps the shells in the trash when he is through. One day, though, he was getting up with the tray of shells in his hand as I walked by and accidentally bumped into him. Shells flew everywhere. I was distressed, but Chris was delighted, because now he could do another favorite activity—vacuum the carpet. I couldn't help but laugh as his face lit up and he said, "I'll get the vacuum!" A sense of humor is a very necessary ingredient in my repertoire for coping.

Unhealthy Humor. Humor, however, can easily become sarcastic, cynical, and nasty. This is obvious when family members play cruel jokes for their own amusement because the child with a disability is so vulnerable.

If parents allow and encourage children to express their true feelings and all emotions are acknowledged, this is less likely to happen. When there is a false sense of harmony, or when feelings have to be repressed, pent-up emotions can leak out in other ways, such as cruel "humor." If real issues are not discussed and "battles" are never fought, a problem-solving process to move toward optimal solutions cannot begin. Unaddressed problems build into pressures, which accumulate to become a volcano of stuffed emotions. These emotions then can explode unexpectedly at "fissures" or events in the family's life.

Negotiation

In a healthy family, parents operate in a mode of negotiation, listening to what everyone has to say and then trying to reach the best possible solution by using everyone's input. Disputes are seen as opportunities to interact and grow, rather than as times when the parents merely act as referees.

Lynn and Jack have three daughters, Sharon, sixteen, Karen, twelve, and Cindy, six, who is mildly retarded and hearing impaired. Lynn would like to pursue a master's degree in social work now that all of the children are in school full time. She can take some classes during the day and also use the girls' school time for studying and library work; but she will need help in caring for Cindy during some late afternoon and evening classes.

If Lynn and Jack can sit down with all three girls and discuss the problem, look at everyone's schedules, and emphasize the benefits of the future degree both to Lynn personally and to the family, negotiation will probably lead to the best possible solution. In this setting, give and take will be done cheerfully and supportively.

In contrast, arbitrarily imposed decisions by any family member may create an eruption that simple discussion could have prevented.

For instance, if Jack does not become a part of the process, if he simply tells Lynn that going to school is okay with him as long as she arranges somehow for childcare, a problem is likely. Or if Lynn announces to Sharon that school begins next week and she's now in charge of the younger girls, that, too, is a problem situation.

A Strong, Shared Faith

In a healthy family, parents have a strong sense of a shared faith that can be clearly stated. Kaslow, writing on characteristics of healthy families, said she had never found a family that scored highly on scales of family health " . . . that does not speak with certainty of a belief in the harmony of the universe, some sense of a Supreme Being or Force in nature, and a humanistic and ethical system of values."[8] For example, she described one family that she considered to be healthy as having children who liked attending church with their parents, and who observed congruence between what the parents said they believed and how they acted in their daily lives.

Since an entire chapter is devoted to the issue of faith and having a child with a disability, I will not deal with it in detail here. However, the issue of faith is a capstone to all of the other characteristics of the healthy family. If the parents are secure in who they are in Christ, then they can allow open communication, negotiation, flexibility, sharing, and expression of emotions; and they can encourage autonomy in their children, disabled and nondisabled alike. For all of this to happen in the home requires an appropriation of the love of Christ and a commitment to love each other as Christ has loved them.

PROBLEM SOLVING STRATEGIES

Once the counselor has been able to see the workings of the family, determine which areas are at risk and which areas require healing, he or she may wish to use the following techniques that relate specifically to families of children with disabilities.

Hulnick and Hulnick outlined a process that may be of benefit to families as they work through some situations. I have chosen six of their recommendations that could become a valuable part of a counselor's array of tools to help a family.[9]

1. *The counselor can help the family reframe the issues so that they can view the situation as a challenge, not as a problem.* Specific questions to use are:

- Can you see any way you can use this situation to your advancement?
- What can you learn from all this?
- What can you do that might result in a more uplifting experience for everyone involved?
- How can you relate to yourself right now in a more loving way? [10]

2. *The family members can be led to take personal responsibility for reaction to the circumstances.* The stressful situation often triggers a deeper emotional problem that requires healing. It is easy for a parent to say that his or her feeling of distress is because of the disability of the child. But this ignores underlying emotions. The family members may be putting themselves into the roles of victims because of outside events. To counter this situation, the counselor should ask the family if there are any alternatives in the situation, and then use the AFA to look at family resources, strengths, and constraints. One clue the counselor can watch for is emotions that continue even when solutions are found—i.e., a general pattern of being upset even when things are going "smoothly."

3. *Family members, and especially parents, should be encouraged to have self-forgiveness and compassion for themselves.* The cause of a developmental disability is not often found. And even if the cause is found, such as oxygen deprivation at birth, it is impossible to target one person as the direct cause of the condition of the child. But some parents take this on, in guilt. Hulnick and Hulnick suggest that an attitude of "only God knows for sure what any disability is all about" will promote emotional health in the parents. This phrase can help them deal with feelings of rage, sadness, loss, and guilt. [11]

4 *The counselor can lead parents to face choices in a healthy manner.* There are many aspects of problem-solving; but the goal is always to reach a solution that will have maximum beneficial results. Two guides for evaluating a family's problem-solving effectiveness are quality, the degree to which family problems are solved, and acceptance, the mutual satisfaction of family members. [12] Two questions, then, to propose to family members are, "How well has this solution solved the problem?" and "How satisfied is each family member with this solution?" The counselor may have to be the one who takes on the role of advocate for the child with the disability in answering these questions.

5. *The counselor can ask the family members questions to empower them by making them aware of their choices.* When the family members realize they do have choices, they will not have feelings of helplessness. They will feel more in control, and, as a result, feel that they have power in the situation to make a difference or a wise choice.

Hulnick and Hulnick propose the following questions to make family members aware of their choices:

- "What choices are you making which tend to perpetuate the problem?
- Are you aware of any other choices you might make which would tend to have a different result? Keep in mind that you are only looking at possibilities and you are not committing to doing anything.
- Let's look at each choice you have brought forward in more detail. What would it really look like if you were to do it? Describe yourself in the present tense as if you are actually doing it now.
- Has considering these questions resulted in any new possibilities for you?"[13]

6. *Teach positive self-talk by asking the family a series of questions and then giving encouragement:*

- "What are you telling yourself about this situation?
- What could you tell yourself right now which would be more self-supporting to you as well as uplifting to your wife (or husband or son, daughter)?
- Would you be willing to begin right now and tell yourself this positive self-talk?
- O. K. Go ahead and do it!"[14]

CONCLUDING THOUGHTS

The family of a child with a disability faces a unique set of stressors that will always be present. The nature of these stressors may change over time; but because the child, and eventually the adult has a permanent condition, the family will always be involved with them in some manner.

Because of the pressures to meet the needs of the family member with the disability, families may be functioning below a healthy level, yet be totally unaware that this is occurring. The strains of daily living may impinge upon the family's state of health in such a gradual, insidious manner that parents and children become caught in a dysfunctional loop without being aware of it. And because the family naturally desires to remain in balance, the dysfunctions are perpetuated, again without awareness.

By focusing on the characteristics of a healthy family presented here, the counselor can hold a standard of functioning up to the family members and allow them to choose where they want to be. Then, by application of the tools presented, he or she can help the family make choices and attain goals. The AFA will help the counselor in assessing the family and defining the areas in which problem-solving must occur. Then the family can learn to prevent problems by using specific problem-solving techniques learned from the counselor. They also can use information to prepare for the future as much as possible, so they are less likely to experience crisis when unexpected events occur.

CHAPTER NINE

A FAITH PERSPECTIVE: SPIRITUAL GROWTH

MAKING SENSE OF A DISABILITY, whether of a child or an adult, presents a theological dilemma for many Christians. By its very nature, a developmental disability is a permanent condition with no rational explanation. It is usually present from birth (even if it is unapparent at first), and therefore it is visited upon the innocent. The cause is usually unknown, generating further confusion for both the person with the disability and especially for the parents.

The counselor who wishes to help families who have children with disabilities must meet personal dilemmas of faith head-on, or else little of value can be accomplished. One's theology is central to one's counseling; a counselor's skills are not used in a sterile framework. We all carry beliefs and attitudes that are reflected in our counseling.

Just as personal attitudes about abortion or homosexuality cannot be totally abandoned when counseling someone on these matters, neither can one's theological position on disability. People who remain disabled throughout life do not fit neatly into a New Testament theology. This causes discomfort in many of us.

EMPATHY AND THE BODY OF CHRIST

It is highly likely that the Christian counselor has a well-developed sense of empathy, which includes the ability to "rejoice with those who rejoice, weep with those who weep" (Rom. 12:15, NAB). If a counselor is overwhelmed by a person's disability, empathy dissolves into sympathy, which is not productive and can lead both counselor and counselee into despair. Sympathy only reinforces the idea of how unfortunate a disability is, and keeps counselees from moving forward, not only in their personal lives, but as members of the body of Christ.

For the Christian counselor, empathy takes on a dimension beyond that of the Rogerian positive regard, or unconditional acceptance of the client. It is based on the concept of being members of the body of Christ, and sharing in his sufferings and in his glory. Not only are the counselor and the family on a journey together through the scheduled sessions, but they are also on a greater journey together toward eternity, where there will be no more crying, no infirmities, and no disabling conditions.

In this context, a mutual understanding and healing can occur. The counselor, in essence, takes on the dual role of discipler and disciple. Counselor and family will learn from each other, and in the process, learn more of the wisdom and grace of God.

FOUR LEVELS OF SPIRITUAL GROWTH

The task in counseling those with disabilities and their families is greater than leading them into problem-solving for practical needs. It is also more than consoling, comforting, and encouraging them. The task is discipleship. Only through discipleship can the person or family be empowered to appropriate the full blessings of God in their lives.

In consolation and in problem-solving, there is attention to immediate needs. In discipleship, there is the foundation for spiritual growth. It is the building of individuals and families who will have the ability to be overcomers, to seek out God's will and power in their lives, and to be witnesses to and encouragers of others. In discipleship, the entire body of Christ benefits. In discipleship, persons are validated as belonging, essential members of the body of Christ.

While the AFA will give an overview of the family's situation and resources, the developmental level of the counselee's Christian walk should also be addressed in order to effectively counsel from a biblical perspective.

The Ivey model of counselee developmental levels mentioned in chapter 5 can be paralleled by levels of spiritual growth portrayed in Scripture: The New Christian (1 Cor. 3:1–4); Beginning Growth (1 John 2:12); Emerging Responsibility (1 John 2:13); and Serving Others, motivated by true love, (1 John 2:14).[1] Jesus' disciples also progressed through stages, from their first call to their full empowerment, changing from people of the world to people of the power of the Holy Spirit. Their development was not on a straight-line progression, however. They were empowered to go out and drive out demons and cure diseases (Luke 9:1), but then the crisis of the crucifixion left them with doubts and fear—which were resolved after the resurrection. Even Peter, to whom Jesus gave the keys of the kingdom, denied Jesus three times in the courtyard of the high priest.

In assessing the counselee's level of spiritual development, it is important to remember that even a person who is others-oriented and spiritually mature can, because of a crisis situation, behave on a lower level. Stress in one area can lead one to operate on a different level of faith.

DISABILITY—GOD'S PUNISHMENT OR GOD'S PLAN?

Disability—Punishment for Sin?

The Christian counselor is intensely aware of the effect of sin—the effect of Adam and Eve's sin on all of us, as well as the effects of personal sin. Much of the suffering of this imperfect world is a result of human rebellion toward God. The Old Testament recollections of plagues and sufferings of the multitudes reinforce this concept. Our modern parade of earthquakes, volcanoes, floods, and wars is a constant reminder of our first parents' rebellion.

Some people carry around the image of a God who punishes us for our personal sin here on this earth. Certainly we know this sin exists, a fact often demonstrated by those who reject God's ways. Murders, rapes, child abuse, robberies, and other terrible crimes fill our TV screens and newspapers each day, attesting to the existence of sin and its consequences, often upon the innocent. But the court system exists so that we can convict and punish the persons responsible for these crimes. If God were in the business of immediate, one-on-one punishment for sin, we would not need courts and jails. Instead God would surely zap criminals immediately and protect the innocent.

Based on childhood experiences, many think of God as an authority figure who favors those who act in socially appropriate ways. Children are told to be good, so that Santa will bring them gifts at Christmas. Schools and Sunday schools often operate on a system of rewards for good behavior. "That's a good girl," or "That's a nice boy," is the response parents give for almost any appropriate behavior—eating, napping, becoming potty trained. Thus, from our toddler days onward, we base our lives on being "good" for those in authority. As adults, we expect that if we are good, that is, if we follow the commandments, obey civic laws, and are loyal to our employers, all will be well in our lives. When we are good, we expect rewards.

Disability, then, doesn't make sense to the person who has this concept of a God who rewards good and punishes evil. People try to fit the disability into a framework to resolve that cognitive dissonance. "What did we do to deserve this?" the parents of a baby with a disability may ask.

In contrast, the Christian counselor, who is to be a conduit of grace and healing to others, cannot ask the question, "What was done to deserve this?" It cannot be asked of God, and certainly cannot be asked of the counselee. The truth is that on our own, none of us deserves anything good. But through redemption by Jesus, we are all heirs to the kingdom, children of the King, and the inheritors of grace.

A disability is not a punishment, any more than nearsightedness is. A disability is, in reality, a temporary condition which will not exist in eternity. The "Why me?" or "Why my child?" questions can never be answered in our own limited, temporal understanding of God's ways—which we know are not our ways. When faith offers explanations, it is no longer faith, but science. When faith can fully explain why each of us is the way we are, and how that fits into God's plan for both planet earth and for eternity, we will no longer need faith.

Disability—Part of God's Plan?

Have you ever looked at a globe, pinpointed your city or town of residence, then looked at it in relation to the entire world? When you do this, you become aware of the immensity of the planet. In that same vein, how many times a day are you consciously aware that you live on a planet, which is part of an immense solar system, which is part of a universe? Not often, right? Most days we are not even consciously aware of the next city, unless we are traveling there. When trying to get to the "Why?" of a disability, it is as though we are trying to comprehend a place beyond our universe. Science can explain a large part of our universe; but the "Why?" part of a disability is known only to God.

Persons' attitudes about having a disability or about being the parent or sibling of a child with a disability can vary widely. Some people's attitudes may not be healthy. They may accept a disability as fate, the luck of the draw, the roll of the dice, or as a punishment for some personal sin. Others may be angry and bitter at God for allowing it to happen. Some may deny the existence of God, because they believe if a loving God existed, he could not allow this to happen. Or a person may take on a martyr-type role, viewing the disability as a cross to bear—a cross from which there is no resurrection.

In contrast, other attitudes can lead to growth and health. The disability may be viewed as a challenge or as an opportunity for personal growth. Some may see the disability as a means of experiencing total dependence on God for provision, and thus they may be graced in a new way. The crisis of disability can generate hope in God's miraculous power, however it may be manifested.

COUNSELOR SELF-AWARENESS OF FAITH ISSUES

It is crucial that the counselor examine his or her own belief system in regard to disability in order to be effective. He or she might use the following questions as a self-check:
- Is my theological position on disability positive, negative, mixed, or unresolved?
- Do I only see problems, or does my approach include a view of the possibilities?
- Am I sufficiently informed of the nature of the person's disability so that I can counsel from a reasonable knowledge base?
- Am I willing to become informed?
- Can I tolerate counselee views of God that are different than my own?
- Can I allow my counselees to express negative emotions at God— anger and rage, or even questioning the existence of God?
- Can I be comfortable when I cannot provide answers and explanations to the counselee?

STEPS IN DISCIPLESHIP

Discipling the individual is a process that has a basic framework, but still allows for individual differences. Discipleship cannot take a cookbook approach with precise recipes that guarantee the exact same results each time they are used. It is more like making a good soup—you take stock of what ingredients you have on hand, add seasonings as necessary, and follow same basic guidelines as to time and cooking temperature. You'll never make the same soup twice.

Similarly, most counselors have a basic "soup recipe" they follow in counseling—a combination of structure and flexibility to work with the individual counselee.

The remaining discussion in this chapter—focusing on assessment, dealing with feelings, understanding healing, acceptance of the disability, forgiveness, and prayer—comprise a "recipe" or guide for discipleship of persons at varying levels of spiritual maturity who are dealing with a seemingly unexplainable disability. Keep in mind that this issue of faith is almost artificially separated out for discussion purposes. Actually, faith is the undergirding of all behavior and counseling interventions. All that is done in counseling should occur through the guidance of the Holy Spirit.

Assessment

First, assess the person's level of spiritual development, and include some discussion about God's role in the disability. Each counselor has a personal style that is unique, so there is no one way to approach this first step. The important thing is that the information is gathered, reflected back to the person, and clear understanding is established.

A counselor may ask, "How do you see God in all of this?" or "What part has your faith had in this circumstance?" He or she might also initiate a discussion of faith by asking, "What is it that helps you cope in this situation?"

Dealing with Feelings

Reassure the counselee that expression of any feeling is allowed, and that it is normal to have mixed feelings. A devoted Christian may rage at God during a distressful crisis situation; he or she may also have feelings of being abandoned by God, or wonder if God has stopped listening. These feelings are human—as humans we are created by God, who also created our range of feelings. The next step once feelings are expressed, is to determine if those feelings are causing problems. If they are leading to dysfunctional behaviors, changes must be made.

The bottom line is that expressing the feelings is acceptable, but remaining stuck in self-defeating or self-destructive behavior is not. The goal is growth, not just learning to live with negative feelings.

Understanding Healing

The counselee's understanding of and attitude toward healing must be established. Among Christians, many varied beliefs about healing exist. Some basic principles about healing should be established later in the counseling relationship, when teaching is appropriate.

Healing does not come through human effort, only through God. He gives the healing where it is most needed, and it can occur in different ways: physically, emotionally, or spiritually. Healing a relationship between a husband and wife or between a parent and child may be more of a priority to God than the physical healing.

The healing may be of a slow, gradual nature that enables the person to achieve God's purposes. When the man was lowered through the roof by his four friends, Jesus forgave him his sins, because he knew that was the man's first need. He then commanded the man to take up his bed and walk as a sign to others (Mark 2:1–12).

A person may be healed spiritually while remaining physically disabled, and thus used mightily by God. *Victorious Survivors* [2] is a moving book about the struggles of young people with disabilities, and of their parents. Many of these children and young adults have experienced serious physical difficulties in addition to mental disabilities. The book contains no reports of healings of the overall condition; but it does describe several miracles that enabled children to successfully come through precarious medical crises. There are also stories of death, but of peaceful death, with God's consolation. Healings of relationships and development of strengths in siblings are also described in these moving stories. Darlene McRoberts, the editor of *Victorious Survivors*, addresses the faith journey of these people. She mentions the blaming of God, the searching of the Scriptures, and the awareness of sickness in the world because of original sin. And then she states, "As we complete our search for the truth, we come face to face with our Savior and Messiah, this time responding by relinquishing our lives and our loved ones to His eternal care."[3] Never did anyone in the Gospels come face to face with Jesus, ask for healing, and be denied. Never. Is not the relinquishing of ourselves and those we love a healing in itself, possibly to be completed in eternity?

Some parents may feel that if only they can get the right person to lay hands on their child and pray, the physical healing will occur. They may take the child around to hear every faith healer who comes into town, or to various prayer meetings, in hopes of finding that one right person who will work the healing. This is somewhat like the parent who takes the child around from doctor to doctor because the diagnosis is not one the parent will accept, although all evidence says that realistically it is the correct diagnosis. If a parent is engaged in searching for the right faith healer, this is the time to offer basic teaching on healing, with God as the source. It should be coupled with strong encouragement to continue praying.

Acceptance of the Disability

The counselee needs to accept the state of his or her condition, or the state of the child's condition. Granted, nothing is impossible for God. But a developmental disability usually remains with a person for life, and acceptance is the first step to opening God's floodgates of blessings. It goes hand in hand with surrendering self and loved ones to God. When we parents can stop the sentences that begin with "If only . . . " and begin to trust God for daily provision, no matter what the body looks like or no matter what state the mind is in, then growth in grace begins.

Paul's second letter to the Corinthians provides an example of recognizing God's grace and provision. Paul suffered continuous persecution almost from the point of his conversion. He was robbed, stoned, beaten, imprisoned, shipwrecked, and eventually martyred. He also suffered anguish from the bickering and in-fighting of members of churches he had established—members who even questioned his fitness to be their leader. Yet Paul never gave up hope; indeed, he counted himself blessed to be persecuted.

Paul recognized the frailty of his own humanity. The paradox of Christianity is that the weak are made strong, not by anything they do, but by the power of God within them. As Paul wrote: "but we have this treasure in earthen vessels, that the excellency of the power may be of God, and not of us" (2 Cor. 4:7, KJV). The New International

Version of the Bible uses "jars of clay" instead of "earthen vessels." The NIV scripture continues:

> We are hard pressed on every side, but not crushed;
> perplexed, but not in despair;
> persecuted, but not abandoned;
> struck down, but not destroyed.
> We always carry around in our body the death of Jesus, so that
> the life of Jesus may also be revealed in our body. (vv 8–10)

The life of Jesus, then, that can be revealed in each of us, cannot be less than total, no matter the condition of the body. John 10:10 states, "I have come that they may have life, and have it to the full." Note there are no "if's" after that verse, no strings are attached. Life in the full is not only for those who can walk, or speak, or hear, or see, or score above 100 on a Stanford-Binet IQ test.

Paul's statement of being content in all circumstances, and the verse that follows, "I can do everything through him who gives me strength" (Phil. 4:12–13) can apply to the circumstance of disability. The contentment, however, may be even more difficult for the parents of the child with a disability. At some point they have to love the child in the present state, turn him or her over to God, and trust for day-to-day provision.

This is a far cry from seeing a punishing God—a God who inflicts burdens, who tests us and tries us and watches with a checklist to see if we can earn our heavenly crown. Accepting the person or self in the current condition to be used by God, to be healed as God sees what healing is needed, is a positive step. Relatives and friends of the person with a disability can become an active part of God's plan. Praying for the person is an integral part of their role, but so is ministering to and caring for this person with the disability for whom God has plans. With that, all involved experience spiritual growth.

In taking the above stance, the counselor is not advising the parent to give up hope of healing. The possibility of God's miraculous intervention is always present. However, while no one can forecast a miracle, the parent can be certain of God's provision for all. Isaiah 49:15 states that even though a mother could forsake the baby at her breast, the Lord promises, "I will not forget you." A nursing mother *cannot* forget about her baby! Even if she suffered a lapse of memory, the milk coming into her breasts at feeding time is a reminder. God's love for a child with a disability is greater even than the mother's love for that child. And God's love for an adult with a disability is greater than any earthly love that person has ever experienced.

Forgiveness

The issue of forgiveness also should be explored in counseling. People may have been hurt along the way by insensitive friends or neighbors, school personnel, or medical professionals. It may have been a putdown, a thoughtless remark or ignoring of needs. Whatever the hurt, it is physically and spiritually healthy for the counselee to be able to forgive others in the spirit of Christ, who forgave his crucifiers because they did not know what they were doing. Even a professional who was expected to be sensitive and knowledgeable may not have been as competent as expected. Or he or she may simply have had a bad day. An offensive statement may have been made from the person's own frustration or lack of understanding, and a caregiver may have reacted with equally offensive words. There is always the possibility that a mistake or an error in judgment was made. No matter the cause, even if it is malicious ill treatment, harboring resentment and unforgiveness is unproductive and potentially harmful to the counselee, and must be worked through.

A person holds on to bitterness and resentment out of fear. He or she has a perception that their refusal to forgive provides them a control—they are, in effect, punishing the offender. Such persons are afraid to forgive because they are afraid to trust God to order their world. They hold onto their anger because they are afraid of the persons they will have to become if they allow themselves to forgive, and eventually, to love. Counselees must forgive themselves of failings, and learn to accept themselves. Then, with a trust in God, they can forgive others.

Sometimes unforgiveness has roots that go beyond the immediate circumstances. The skilled counselor will be able to discover whether this person is actually angry over other events. At that point, past unresolved issues must be resolved as they would in any counseling setting.

The counselor must show the person how harboring unforgiveness is harmful because it requires a great deal of emotional energy and time. An unforgiving person must maintain a mental list of who is loved and who is not, and then always act accordingly. This requires physical energy, because, with the mental recall of the unforgiven person, the brain releases hormones that accompany the stressful anger reaction, which may lower the body's resistance to infection by suppressing the immune system.

Hans Selye documented the effect of intense emotions on the body in his development of the concept of the GAS (General Adaptation Syndrome), the body's reaction to stress.[4] Newer research has revealed subtle differences in the body's reaction to different stressors. However, the vast majority of medical experts agree with the basic premises of Selye's forty years of research, that prolonged stress produces physical deterioration. Recent studies confirm Selye's work and have focused on persons' reactions to catastrophe, significant life changes, and daily hassles, emphasizing our perceptions and interpretations of those events as determinants of harm to the body.[5]

Unforgiveness also blocks relationships. The person who has unforgiveness in his or her life cannot be free and open with others. All people become suspect because they will have to eventually be placed in a category of loved or hated.

Lastly, unforgiveness blocks the relationship with God. We know well the exhortation in Matthew 5:23 that we are to set matters right with others before we bring our gifts to the altar. The counselee may also need to ask forgiveness of others for his or her reactions in circumstances that may have alienated or offended them. There are many Christian books on forgiveness that might be recommended to counselees.[6]

Prayer

Christian discipleship cannot occur without prayer. Its place in the counseling process has been discussed by many Christian authors.[7] Books on prayer and healing also can be of value to both counselor and counselees.[8]

Prayer encompasses a wide continuum of forms and methods. Many Christian counselors begin or end counseling sessions with prayer. Other counselors prefer to pray privately before or after they see the counselees. Prayer also may be a brief time, with the counselee present, of asking for guidance at the beginning of a session and for blessing at the end. The counselor may join hands with the counselee during prayer. Or, depending on the counselor's theological position, there may be laying on of hands, or anointing for healing. The counselor may structure time at the end of the session for extensive prayer.

Two further observations are offered about prayer. The first is that prayer spoken aloud can be especially beneficial. When a person hears prayer spoken in his or her behalf by another, it reinforces the idea of being valued. Prayer spoken aloud also keeps hope alive in both the counselee and the counselor, and is as much for the benefit of counselor as the counselee. Prayer gives hope where hope sometimes does not seem to exist.

The counselor should consider the condition of the person being prayed for. If the person is hearing impaired or deaf, ask someone to sign the prayer. If the person is an infant, or in a coma, praying words of hope aloud may be essential. Recent evidence suggests that patients under anesthesia have a better rate of recovery when they hear positive messages played on tapes during surgery.[9] It may be possible that those who seemingly do not respond physically can respond mentally and spiritually to spoken prayer and Scripture. In addition, relatives of the baby or adult with a disability can gain hope from hearing these words.

The second observation is that the counselor should always keep in mind the preferences of the counselee regarding prayer. Some prefer silent prayer, while others need to have prayers spoken aloud. If the counselor prefers to pray in tongues and the counselee is not receptive to this mode of prayer, the prayer may then become a stumbling block, rather than an avenue toward healing. If the counselor prefers to hold someone's hand while praying, to lay hands on the person, or to anoint him or her and pray for healing, permission should be asked first of the person, or parent of the child. These attitudes and beliefs of the counselee should always be respected.

God recognizes many kinds of prayer; we do not have to act according to a particular formula. The important thing is that the counselee's needs are met. Of course, there is always the possibility of a reverse situation occurring. The counselee may prefer some method of prayer that the counselor may be disinclined to use because of his or her theology or level of discomfort. This is a matter between the counselor and God, and openness is highly recommended.

THE MINISTRY OF THOSE WITH DISABILITIES

When a person has reached the stage of acceptance of the current physical and/or mental condition, the next stage begins to unfold. That stage is being open to what God has in mind for that person in his perfect plan.

A jar is not meant to be stashed away in a closet. A jar is to be used for functional or decorative purposes. It has a reason to exist. "In a large house there are articles not only of gold and silver, but also of wood and clay" (2 Tim. 2:2). Other translations substitute the words "vessels" or "dishes" for "articles." To paraphrase the lines that follow, some are for great occasions, and some are for ordinary use or menial service; but all have the potential to be an instrument for honorable purposes, for noble use, in the service of the master of the household. They remain ready for all good service, for all honorable employment.

No matter what the exterior, all of these jars or dishes or vessels are to be used. Similarly, all of us are to be used in the Master's service. The only condition attached to these verses in Timothy is to keep clean, and to stay away from what is ignoble and evil. The Scriptures do not require a perfect body and/or mind.

Joni Eareckson Tada is an example of a vessel who is used by God to reach people all over the world. The condition of her body is incidental to God's purposes. Skip Wilkins from Virginia Beach, Virginia, is a superb wheelchair athlete and a nationally recognized Christian motivational speaker. You probably can also add the names of people you know who minister through their disabilities.

It is easier to comprehend how someone with impaired body but sound mind can minister to others than it is to understand how someone with mental disability can do this. The ministry then becomes nonverbal. Those with mental disabilities minister by giving love, warmth, and acceptance to all of us. They trust us completely to meet their needs, and they cause us to examine our values—and in some instances, to change our lives.

You can learn this through conversations with teachers in special education, teen volunteers at special camps, and members of community organizations who volunteer time and money to those with disabilities. After five minutes with Bob Miller, director of Special Olympics in Virginia Beach, you will know, without his telling you, of his love for his "folks," as he calls his special athletes. When Bob speaks in public, he tells of how their love changed his life. He thought he knew about Christian love, he says until he worked with the special athletes and found out what the love of Christ was all about.

In *The Road to Daybreak*,[10] Henri Nouwen tells of the year he spent with Jean Vanier in Trosly, which led to his becoming a member of the L'Arche community, Daybreak, in Toronto. This book, which is a journal of that year, deals with many topics, from prayer to art to AIDS. Many entries are about the residents of L'Arche homes, and how the author's life has been affected by these people with disabilities. He talks about the "gift of the handicapped," writing, "They see through a facade of smiles and friendly words and sense the resentful heart before we ourselves notice it. . . . For them, what counts is a true relationship, a real friendship, a faithful presence. . . . Being at L'Arche means many things, but one of them is a call to a greater purity of heart." [11]

Nouwen also remarks that " . . . the most unlikely people are chosen by God to make us see." [12] In the epilogue of the book, which he wrote a year after becoming resident priest at Daybreak, he discusses the "second loneliness, . . . that asks of me to throw myself completely into the arms of a God whose presence can no longer be felt and to risk every part of my being to what seems like nothingness." This second loneliness, he writes, is " . . . following Jesus to a completely unknown place." [13]

Reading these words, I feel that as a parent, I too have experienced this second loneliness. Nouwen speaks of it as his own personal acceptance in community, and experiencing Jesus in community. I have experienced it as having to accept my son's life, and so often having to commit everything to God. It is also having the rest of the world sometimes accept, and sometimes reject, you and your child.

Much about the life of a child with a disability will be unknown, and many times it is as though one walks in the dark, and has to rely on the Divine for light, for no other light is available. Often I have had to be vulnerable to Christopher's world, where education, position, and title mean nothing—where all that matters is God's love.

SOME CONCLUDING THOUGHTS

We have all experienced times in our lives when we felt far away from God, and other times when we felt so close that his presence seemed to surround us. We have known times of spiritual ecstasy and abject agony. There have been days when we wonder if any of the Bible makes sense, or perhaps even wrestled with the whole notion of if there is really a God. And there have been days when it all seems to make perfect sense—days of miracles and wonders. Philip Yancy explores this theme in his book, *Disappointment With God.* [14]

And so it will be with those who seek counseling. The disability of the person or of a loved one may be a stressor or a blessing. It can be a factor in plunging a person into the depths of despair, or a vehicle to lift someone to experience God in a new and exciting way. It can be an occasion for doubt or a point of conversion. Most likely, elements of all these possibilities will occur at different times in the counselee's life.

The assessment of the counselee's level of spiritual development begins the process of discipling according to needs. Ideally, the counselor who performs this assessment will be spiritually mature. It is crucial for the counselor to be able to assess his or her own level of spiritual development in order to relate his or her own concepts of God, of sin and of healing to persons with disabilities and their families. Honesty about personal beliefs and values will assist the counselor in being empathic, that is, in understanding the needs, issues, and feelings of the counselee, with a goal of discipling. In this way, the counselor will be doing much more than reflecting feelings and solving problems. He or she will be leading the counselees to become full heirs in the kingdom of heaven.

CHAPTER TEN

THE CHURCH'S MINISTRY
TO THOSE WITH DISABILITIES

IF THEY KNEW WHAT TO DO and how to do it, churches would have more ministries to those who have disabilities and their families. I have heard pastors and lay leaders say they desire to serve these people, but they do not know where to begin.

Their concerns are sincere—and their doubts are valid. Sometimes they don't know where to begin because this population is "hidden," not seen in church, Sunday school, or in the youth group. The family members may not be active participants on church committees. Additionally, church leaders may feel overwhelmed at the prospect of serving those with disabilities, fearing that they lack the necessary expertise and might cause harm, or not wanting to say or do something that might offend the family.

This combination of being unaware and feeling unequipped is often the barrier which prevents ministry to those with disabilities in the church. Neither of these problems is insurmountable, however. Effective ministry is possible; but it requires dedicated leadership from caring people who will make a commitment to serve in this realm.

BASIC ELEMENTS OF PASTORAL CARE

Pastoral care for families affected by disability does not require extraordinary efforts, but rather an extension of skills that already exist.[1]

Knowledge

Caring must be accompanied by basic knowledge; competence is necessary for a constructive response to people's problems. But this knowledge does not mean advanced degrees or extra college courses. Acquiring knowledge to help families is not a difficult task; it can be gained through many ways:

- Reading some basic books on mental and/or physical disabilities
- Skimming the local newspapers for news of support groups and seminars
- Becoming aware of community resources for referral for services
- Making contact with agencies and institutions that can provide information on request, such as the March of Dimes or a medical school library
- Discussing issues with church members who are in the medical field or who are special education teachers
- Asking the family directly to help you gain greater knowledge and understanding. Families are usually glad to share specific details about their children and their disabilities.

The Capacity for Self-Evaluation

A counselor must always be open to self-evaluation so that personal growth can continue. In interacting with families who have members with disabilities, these questions for self-examination will facilitate evaluation and growth:

- Did I feel uncomfortable meeting with this family? If so, why? What can I do about this discomfort?
- What was my own behavior in relationship to the person(s) I was trying to help?

- What did I do that was helpful?
- What was missing in how I responded?
- Did I face the family members and their concerns openly, or did I shy away because I felt incompetent or unconcerned about the disability?

Patience

A counselor or pastor may feel discouraged when a counselee does not progress according to the counselor's schedule. Sometimes it is difficult to understand why a counselee does not follow through with a matter that is seemingly simple. For example, a counselor may refer parents to a community service for the child, and then find out a month later that they have not followed up by calling for the service. The counselor in this case may then feel unappreciated, and he or she may judge the family as being unresponsive to help. But neither reaction is helpful. A family must be allowed its own time and space for solving problems, even when direct help is given.

Instead of being critical of the parents, the counselor may ask if they are having some difficulties in connecting with that service, and then offering to assist in a problem-solving process, if that is necessary.

Trust in the Holy Spirit

Trust in the Holy Spirit must also be a part of pastoral care. The counselor or pastor must trust that the Holy Spirit will lead and that guidance and answers to prayers will come in God's perfect timing.

Part of that trust means being open to discernment of the difference between overprotection of counselees and an appropriate outreach. In the earlier example, the parents may have had a number of reasons why they did not contact the community service: They may have needed transportation or baby-sitting; they may have felt intimidated by professionals and did not want to approach the agency on their own; or they may not have been able to read the agency brochure that was given to them. In any of those circumstances, more help would be required from the church.

Honesty

Honesty is an element of the self-evaluation mentioned earlier. It also means being realistic about the nature of the disability of the child and what is actually happening in the family. It is so easy to "super-spiritualize" the family, to gloss over the reality because of the counselor's need to have a "wonderful" Christian family with a "witness" to others. But this denies the actual circumstances of the family members and does not allow the church to reach out to them.

Humility

Knowing our own limits enables us to provide better services to others. Knowing their limitations allows counselors and pastors to refer counselees to competent others without feeling guilty because they could not meet all of the needs, themselves. It also allows counselors to consult with others who may be able to give additional insights or information. A counselor may mistakenly lead counselees to believe that only he or she can solve their problems. This is a prideful attitude that promotes dependency and inhibits the counselees' growth.

Hope

Christian hope means waiting patiently for what we do not yet have (Rom. 8:25). This hope is the essence of churches and pastoral care. Such caring for another is, ". . . an expression of the whole life and purpose of the Christian community."[2] It is especially significant for those with disabilities. Often, situations will seem hopeless when viewed with our natural eyes. But if we recognize that Christ is our hope (Col. 1:27), we know that our circumstances, both temporal and eternal, are in God's hands.

Courage

Courage is a necessary prerequisite to hope, because it takes courage to offer help and healing to others as a representative of Christ and of the church community. It takes courage to put ourselves forward and work with those in stress and in crisis. It takes courage to continue to hold out hope to others, balancing faith and humility.

THE PASTOR AS KEY TO MINISTRY

The pastor is not the church; the people are the church, and the pastor is their shepherd and leader. This does not mean, however, that pastors have to take the role as leaders in actually establishing ministries for those with disabilities and their families. But their attitudes and their encouragement of others in this task will be crucial to such a ministry. Pastors can lead and guide those who would directly minister; and they can lead the entire congregation in being more aware and accepting of those with disabilities. In this the counselor can be a valuable resource to the pastor, both as a source of information about disabilities and related needs, and as an encourager to become active in meeting needs.

Teaching

The pastor has powerful tools to facilitate a climate in the church that will lead to a ministry for those with disabilities. One of the most powerful tools is teaching from the pulpit. However, it is rare today to hear a pastor discuss the topic of those with permanent disabilities in a Sunday sermon. Outside of readings from the Gospel that relate miracles affecting those with illnesses and afflictions, little solid theology is offered regarding disabilities.

If a church takes a stand against abortion, the church then has an obligation to take a concomitant stand to be pro-life for all, supporting those with disabilities. The attitude proclaimed by the pastor can be crucial in the congregation's growth of understanding. A view of God that treats all life as sacred and of value is one that will convey to those with disabilities and their families that there is purpose to their lives and that they have access to being empowered in Christ.[3]

Administration

The pastor can encourage a welcoming spirit in the church by making the church physically hospitable. Public buildings are supposed to be accessible for those with disabilities, but in reality there is usually no place in the rows of church pews for a wheelchair or a child's stroller to fit without jutting out into the aisle. Ramps may not exist, or they may be too steep, and restrooms may not be accessible.

The Americans with Disabilities Act, which was signed into law by President Bush in 1990, provides that all buildings that are open to the public will have to accommodate those in wheelchairs, provided the cost is not excessive. However, Section 307 of the act exempts churches from meeting this requirement.

Another way to increase awareness of those with disabilities is to encourage their participation in church services. Perhaps few church councils have attempted to actively include those with disabilities as ushers, in children's choir, or in other serving capacities. There are places to serve for those with both mental and physical disabilities.

STARTING A MINISTRY TO THOSE WITH DISABILITIES

Two formal documents give a mandate to the local church to serve those with disabilities. The first is the *Pastoral Statement of U.S. Catholic Bishops on People with Disabilities, November 16, 1978.* This document begins, "The same Jesus who heard the cry for recognition from the people with disabilities of Judea and Samaria 2,000 years ago calls us, His followers, to embrace our responsibility to our own disabled brothers and sisters in the United States."

The document contains thirty-five paragraphs, and deals with many aspects of disability, including prejudice, the biblical basis for this ministry, full participation in the Christian community, and the recognition of the importance of family members in the life of the person with the disability. A copy of the document can be obtained from the National Catholic Office for Persons with Disabilities (see Appendix II for the address).

In March 1989, the National Association of Evangelicals passed a resolution on ministries to persons with disabilities at its annual convention. The resolution calls upon churches to reach out to those with disabilities and welcome them in the life of the church in an active manner, including providing leadership to minister effectively to them. Many of the groups who formed this resolution have also formed a Christian Council on Persons with Disabilities, led by Joni Eareckson Tada and The Christian Fund for the Disabled. A copy of the full resolution and further information are available from Joni and Friends (see Appendix II).

Whom Do We Serve?

Although these two documents exist, with the Catholic Bishops' Statement predating that of the Evangelicals by more than ten years, there are few precedents for churches to follow in providing services to families who have children with disabilities. It is only in the past fifteen years, with passage of PL 94–142, that these children have been, for the most part, reared at home while attending local schools, rather than being institutionalized as they were in the past.

Most of the focus in church programming has followed the special education movement and developed curricula and special classes for religious education in the form of Bible studies and Sunday school classes. There is a place for these activities; but a church with only this type of program for children with special needs unintentionally but totally ignores the family that brings the child to the classes.

A Sunday school teacher's function is to be with that child for an hour a week, with no provision for the rest of the family. Often we do not see that this Sunday school class may be that family's one connection with the church. When this happens, the church is missing an opportunity for ministry to that family, who may not even be members of the congregation.

The more likely situation is that the family does not bring this child to church because of difficulties of behavior, physical accommodations, or condition of the child. Family members may share childcare duties and attend different services. The entire family may not have ever been seen in church at one time, and no one may be aware that there is a child with a disability.

Because of the demands of care for the child, the parents may not be able to serve on any church committees or in any ministry, and therefore no one really knows this family. This is particularly true for a church with a large congregation, where many people are strangers to one another.

Assessing Needs

The church that is committed to having a ministry to those with disabilities and their families must begin with an assessment of needs. The first step is to find out who in the congregation has a family member with a disability. This can be accomplished in several ways; using a combination of methods will produce the most valid results.

- An announcement can be made periodically from the pulpit to encourage people to let the pastor know about those with special needs, especially those families who have children with disabilities.
- A regular notice can be placed in the bulletin to remind people of the church's desire to know about those children with disabilities so that services can be provided. This is especially crucial for newborns, those children who are newly diagnosed, and those who have just moved into the area.
- The church can conduct a survey, either at a church service or by mail, to establish which families have members with disabilities. It might be effective to have people fill out this form at services on three consecutive Sundays to ensure that the majority of those who regularly attend church are included in the survey.

- The registration cards that many churches have in the pews or give out to those who are attending for the first time can carry a line asking whether there are any persons with disabilities in the family. It can also include a space for the family to request further contact for support services.

What Services Are Needed?

The basis for developing a ministry to families who have members with disabilities could be considered from three perspectives:

- What do these families need from the church?
- What does having a family member with a disability do to the family's ability to attend church services and to participate in the life of the church?
- How can the church reach out to those families who are not church members, or who have family members who are not believers?

The answers to these questions will vary from church to church, but will probably include some common answers, too. All families share in some basic needs, such as respite care. Churches differ in size and resources, so what can actually be provided will be different, too, depending upon the church's circumstances. When approached from two levels, ministry to those with disabilities can be addressed in a manner so that all churches can provide at least some services.

The first level is that of the individual church, and may or may not involve actual programs. The second is that of forming a consortium of churches so that resources may be pooled. What is common to all churches, large or small, rural, urban, or suburban, mainline or non-denominational, is that these families need the church. It is within the framework of the church that the family can express their faith, sustain their hopes, and experience the love of God as others demonstrate it to them.

The Individual Church. A foundational ministry of the individual church is developing a policy so that it will not only receive but will welcome those with disabilities into the congregation. It is a natural tendency to fear those whom we perceive as suffering, especially those for whom we feel we can do nothing.[4] This is one reason we are uncomfortable with those who have disabilities—their needs are visible.

155

We feel inept because we think that to be of help to them we must be some kind of a super person and that helping will require an extraordinary effort on our part.

What is actually required is the necessity to feel free just ". . . to be with, to be present to"[5] those who have a disability. Doing comes after being. The realization that we share the same joys and fears as those with disabilities must come first. This may sound like a simple step, but it is not only first, it is foundational and ongoing. As Jean Vanier wrote, "It is easy to be generous for a few months or even years. But to be continually present to others and not only present but nourishing, to keep going in a fidelity which is reborn each morning, demands a discipline of body and spirit."[6]

The church might begin by finding those who have needs, welcoming them in, and learning just to be with these families as they are present in the congregation. This is an important step for all concerned, because families who have children with disabilities may stay away from church because of past negative experiences. Parents truly suffer from misperceptions and judgments of others about their children with disabilities.

Many well-meaning Christians do not understand what it is like to be the parent of a child with a developmental disability. They sometimes try to explain away what is not understandable. Or they may use trite expressions because their discomfort will not allow them to discuss the issue in any other way. Parents of children with disabilities often hear statements from church members such as these: "What saints you parents are to take care of this child," or "You are a marvelous example to all of us," or "You must be a very special person to be chosen by God for this burden," or finally, "Your heavenly crown must have many jewels."

Some church members may question the faith of parents of a child who is not healed of a disability, suggesting that they are not praying hard enough, not claiming God's promises, or not "standing on the Word" (whatever that may mean). Parents may dread being in a situation where misguided Christians believe that a miracle will come if only "this time" we lay hands on this child and pray for healing.

Another particularly insidious strategy is for someone to suggest that there must be unrepented sin in someone's life for healing not to have come about. I have a friend with a disability who told me that she has been subject to all of these tactics over and over again in her life.

Sound teaching from the pulpit can dispel these false beliefs in a congregation and can give a balanced perspective on prayer and healing.

Some of the ways a congregation can focus on being present to others are simple, and can apply to a church of fifty or five hundred. The first is by a conscious reaching out, as mentioned earlier, to locate those with disabilities. A church could also contact community agencies, particularly those with group homes, and let it be known that those with disabilities are welcome.

Individual members might be willing to provide transportation for those with disabilities who would like to attend services or other activities. The church could also make a concerted effort to contact these families when there are church functions such as suppers, picnics, plays, or fairs, and ask what help they might need to be able to attend and enjoy the event.

In addition, there could be a commitment to prayer support for those with disabilities. A liturgical church can include these petitions in a formal manner. Some members may want to make a personal commitment to pray for the families daily; others may offer to come and pray with them on a regular basis.

In today's mobile society, many of these families are not living near their family of origin. In this case, the church network could provide extended "family." Families who have children with disabilities need love and acceptance by other families. They would welcome church members who could be the aunts, uncles, cousins, and grandparents who live so far away and who are so seldom seen. Even if the relatives of these families are geographically close, very often there is an emotional distancing so there is a need for support.

The philosophy of the individual church should be of inclusion of children with disabilities and their families in the life of the church. Meeting individual needs should be balanced with community participation. An example of this is to have children with special needs attend regular Sunday school classes with a buddy system so that each child has a peer in the class to help guide and instruct. For teens with disabilities this is especially valuable, for no teen-ager wants to sit in a class of little children.

Continual segregation, at school and at church, is not conducive toward developing needed social skills. To be accepted by one's peers, regardless of IQ, adds to self-esteem. What better place to demonstrate loving acceptance by peers than in the church setting?

A Consortium Approach. The task of meeting the needs of families who have children with disabilities probably cannot, in reality, be accomplished by any one church, acting singularly. There are at least two reasons for this: The needs are many, and the numbers of children with disabilities in any one church is likely to be a small percentage of the total congregation. However, churches could band together and form a consortium that would provide a variety of services for more people.

In most places, several churches of various denominations are in close proximity. Where I live, for example, the following churches are clustered within two miles of each other: Roman Catholic, Presbyterian, Methodist, Lutheran, Episcopal, Baptist, and a non-denominational. These churches probably represent a membership of three to four thousand families. There are probably four hundred families in this area who have a family member with a disability. About one-fourth of those persons are probably children. Even if the numbers were such that only fifty families had a child with a disability, no one of these churches could provide all needed services; but a consortium approach could be of service to all.

A consortium could work in one of two ways: either a central board could be formed with services provided from pooling members from all churches, with physical locations for specific services in certain churches, or each church could exclusively operate in one or two functions. Besides counseling, some of the needs of parents that could be addressed by churches are: respite care, parent support groups, training, sibling support groups, grandparent support groups, resource information, behavioral training, and Bible instruction for children with disabilities.

Cooperation with local agencies and services is another mode of consortium functioning. Existing services could be expanded if churches provided volunteers and site locations for programs. In addition, a Christian component could be developed in programs for parents. This could be prayer, support groups, teaching, Bible study, counseling, healing services, or other programs that the churches could offer. If these distinctively Christian components were not tied into any public funding, and kept separate from the program itself, but available to those who expressed interest, there would be no conflict of interests.

The church is in a position to reclaim service in areas that it has abandoned to the public sector. Human services, particularly to those dependent populations such as the ill and infirm, were originally provided by the church, but later abandoned to government.[7] We are dealing with tough problems in our society—homelessness, addiction, the increase of poverty among children, the increase of single-parent families. We have delegated governmental structures to provide for those in need, and as a result, we are seeing wider gaps in our society between the haves and have-nots. As Joni Eareckson Tada stated, ". . . good theology must be accompanied by good sociology."[8] The church must strike a balance between evangelization and outreach if it sincerely believes the gospel message it teaches. Christian counselors who work with disabled persons and their families will be most effective when they work in partnership with caring, sensitive members of local churches.

ANNOTATED FAMILY APPRAISAL

(Appendix I may be photocopied for your use.)

Family name _____

Name and age of each immediate family member:

_____ _____ _____

_____ _____ _____

Name and age of other significant extended-family members:

_____ _____ _____

_____ _____ _____

A. The Event

1. Immediate presenting problem:
   _pregnant, expecting child with a disability

_birth of child with disability
_diagnosis just received of child with disability
_problems with child who has known diagnosis
_recent accident or illness causing disability
_other family problems

2. Nature of child's disability:
_known diagnosis
_genetic causation
_limitations
_abilities
_behaviors
_approximate age level of functioning
_medical involvement
_child on medication
_child in school and/or treatment program

3. Source of the problem:
_unable to attain needed diagnosis
_school-related
_physical illness or debilitation
_critical transition for child (beginning or ending school, job, residential situation)
_home behavior

4. Other events occurring in the family presently or recently:
_separation
_divorce
_death
_a sibling leaving home (college, military, marriage, job)
_parent away from home because of job (include military)
siblings with serious problems
_addition of household members
_serious illness of other family members
_remarriage
_new stepsiblings
_financial changes in family
_alcohol or other substance abuse in family member
_incarceration of family member
_family member placed in residential setting
_recent disaster—fire, car accident, etc.
_significant parental career change
_move of family home
_change in church membership/attendance
_change in social activities

B. Family Resources

1. Ability of family to meet its financial obligations
   _general financial health of family (assets minus liabilities)
2. Social support systems
   _extended family in area
   _extended family out of area
   _support from father's family
   _support from mother's family
   _support from church members
   _support from neighbors
3. Faith
   _family's statement of level of faith
   _existence of individual and family prayer
   _church membership
   _church attendance
4. Knowledge/utilization of community resources
   _respite care in home
   _respite care overnight or for vacation
   _recreation
   _schools/special education programs
   _school-related parent-resource center
   _special education advisory committee
   _infant stimulation programs
   _preschool
   _specialized preschool
   _after-school community programs
   _Special Olympics (if retardation is present)
   _national support organizations
   _medical/genetic information on specific disorder
   _physical therapy
   _speech therapy
   _occupational therapy
   _summer camps and programs
   _church-related programs—Sunday school, nursery care, sacrament
   preparation before baptism, communion, confirmation, etc.
   _parent support groups, local
   _parenting-skills groups
   _sibling support groups
   _community advocacy
   _vocational training/rehabilitation programs
   _supported-employment programs

_residential programs in the community
 SCNF (skilled-care nursing facility)
 ICF (intermediate care facility)
 independent living
 supported independent living
 group homes
_transportation
_SSI and Medicaid
_residential schools
_residential vocational-training schools
_specialized medical care
_dentist for special-needs children or adults

C. What Is the Family's Definition of the Event

1. What is the emotional state of the family and of each family member?
2. Are there any signs that the family feels overwhelmed, such as a general inability to cope?
3. Are they ready to meet this challenge but need help to do so?
4. What is the view of each family member of this situation?
5. What is the view of the person with the disability (if applicable)?
6. Are there extended family members who are significantly close (either physically or emotionally) to the family whose views are essential to the family?
7. What is the level of acceptance of the child's disability by each family member? by the family as a whole?
8. How do the family members define the event in terms of their faith?

D. Previous Problem-Solving

1. What have been the significant problems for this family in the past?
2. What have been problems that specifically involved the child's disability?
3. How were these problems resolved?
   Who took responsibility for solution?
   What would have been done differently?
   What was learned in the past situation that is applicable in the future?
4. What abilities/talents does each family member have that can be applied in solving problems?
5. What is needed for the family to resolve future problems more effectively?
6. What was the family of origin like for each parent?
   What is the genogram, or family tree, for each parent?

7. Are there unresolved issues that individual family members need to explore in a therapeutic framework?
couple/marital issues?
sibling/parental issues?

E. Readiness

1. What stage(s) of family life is (are) now occurring?
List all critical transitions that may apply for each member.
2. What task(s) is (are) immediately facing the family (from the family's point of view)?
What unnamed tasks do you, the counselor, perceive as facing the family?
What has the family done regarding these immediate tasks?
3. What predictable events are in the future for the child with a disability?
Which of these predictable events has the family recognized as being of concern?
In which predictable event does the family feel that they will be able to have control in the decision-making process that will be involved?
Which factors does the family feel it will be unable to control?
Are any of these possibly controllable?
What steps will have to be taken to move the family into the area of having control?
Is the family willing to prepare?
Is the family able to prepare?
What additional resources are necessary for preparation?

APPENDIX II

RESOURCES

Books for Further Reading
From Miscellaneous Sources:

See the chapter footnotes for books that are of special interest, such as *Before and After Zachariah,* by Fern Kupfer; *Victorious Survivors,* edited by Darlene McRoberts; and *Families of Handicapped Children,* edited by Rebecca R. Fewell and Patricia F. Vadasy.

The Boston University Bookstore has a division called the Exceptional Parent Library which carries a variety of books from many publishers that deal with disabilities of children and adults, as well as books for parents. The address is 600 Beacon Street, Boston, MA 02215; phone 617-267-8484.

Brookline Books publishes a number of books for children and adults with disabilities, including books about advocacy. The address is P.O. Box 1046, Cambridge, MA 02238; phone 617-868-1772.

Specific Recommended Titles:

Winifred Anderson, Stephen Chitwood, and Diedre Hayden, *Negotiating the Special Education Maze: A Guide for Parents and Teachers,* 2d ed. (Rockville, MD: Woodbine House, 1990). This is a definitive, specific guide that helps make sense of the often-confusing special education system. It is informative and complete, with appendices containing extensive directories of federal, state, and private offices, and organizations for children and adults.

Helen Featherstone, *A Difference in the Family: Life With a Disabled Child* (New York: Basic Books, 1982). The author is a parent and a teacher who writes of her personal experiences. Parents will identify with her, and professionals will gain a real understanding of special-needs parents.

Interfaith Volunteer Caregiving: A Special Report, presents a model for community-based caregiving by lay persons for elderly and those with disabilities. Free copies are available from The Robert Wood Johnson Foundation, P.O. Box 2316, Princeton, NJ 08543-2316.

Bill Clarke, S.J. *Enough Room for Joy: Jean Vanier's L'Arche; A Message for Our Time* (New York: Paulist Press, 1974). Describes the beginnings of L'Arche.

Michael Downey. *A Blessed Weakness* (New York: Harper and Row, 1986). This book is a biography of Jean Vanier.

From Paul Brookes Publishing Co.

Paul H. Brookes Publishing Company (P.O. Box 10624, Baltimore, MD 21285-0624; phone 1-800-638-3775) publishes the bulk of books on the market today that deal with disabilities of children and adults. It regularly mails announcements of books in this field, and both parents and professionals can be on its mailing list. Samples of books which may be of interest are:

Mark L. Batshaw and Yvonne M. Perret, *Children with Handicaps: A Medical Primer,* 2d ed. (1986). This is a textbook-like, comprehensive book for both parents and professionals. It thoroughly discusses many disabilities, and is an excellent reference book.

Debra J. Lobato, *Brothers, Sisters, and Special Needs* (1990). This is a curriculum and activity guide for children ages three to eight who have siblings with developmental disabilities or chronic illnesses. A *Leader's Companion Packet* is also available for conducting a sibling workshop program.

Thomas H. Powell and Peggy Ahrenhold Ogle. *Brothers and Sisters—A Special Part of Exceptional Families* (1985). This is a book for parents and professionals on the special needs of siblings of children and adults with disabilities. Both counseling and parental strategies are included.

Siegfried M. Pueschel, ed. *A Parent's Guide to Down Syndrome* (1990). This book is written with a life-span approach to help parents from birth of the child through transition into adulthood. Dr. Pueschel has authored several excellent books on Down syndrome.

Siegfried M. Pueschel, James C. Bernier, and Leslie Weidenman, *The Special Child: A Source Book for Parents of Children with Developmental Disabilities* (1988). This book offers practical advice for parents on a wide range of issues such as legal, education, medical, and adaptive equipment.

H. Rutherford Turnbull, et al., *Disability and the Family: A Guide to Decisions for Adulthood* (1989). A hands-on approach for parents, this book suggests specific strategies for making decisions about the future of the young adult with a disability, and contains references and worksheets.

Books by Jean Vanier from Paulist Press, Mahway, New Jersey:

Man and Woman He Made Them (1984)
The Challenge of L'Arche (1982)
Community and Growth (1979)
Be Not Afraid (1975)
The Broken Body (1988)
I Meet Jesus: He Tells Me "I Love You" (1982)
I Walk with Jesus (1986)
Also: *In Weakness, Strength; The Spiritual Sources of Georges P. Vanier, 19th Governor-General of Canada* (Toronto: Griffin House, 1969).

From Government Publishers:

The United States government offers many publications that are available at no cost to parents and professionals. The following directories and bibliographies provide comprehensive information about both services and publications.

Clinical Programs for Mentally Retarded Children, DHHS Publication No. (HRSA) HRS-D-MC 85-1, U.S. Department of Health and Human Services, Division of Maternal and Child Health, Rockville, MD 20057. This publication lists outpatient medical facilties in the United States and its territories that provide evaluation, treatment, and follow-up services for children with mental retardation and other developmental disabilities. Generally, they serve children from birth to age twenty-one.

The following publications are available from the National Center for Maternal and Child Health Clearinghouse, 38th and R Streets N.W., Washington, DC 20057; phone 202-625-8400 or 8410:

Reaching Out: A Directory of National Organizations Related to Maternal and Child Health (March 1989). This is a valuable reference guide to organizations throughout the United States, both public and private nonprofit, that serve children and adults with a very broad range of disabilities.

Resources for Clergy in Human Genetics Problems: A Selected Bibliography, 2d ed. (1988). This is a bibliography covering topics from bioethics and genetics to legal and moral issues in order to introduce pastors, pastoral case workers, and educators to counseling aspects of genetics and birth defects treatment issues.

Starting Early: A Guide to Federal Resources in Maternal and Child Health. This comprehensive listing includes federal agencies and information centers, publications, and audio-visual materials (many available at no cost for single copies), and regional medical and genetic services. Foreign-language publications are also included.

Periodicals:

Exceptional Parent is a publication that is invaluable to both parents and professionals. The articles offer practical information about dealing with specific issues regarding children and adults with both mental and physical disabilities. Regular features include book reviews, a family case study, information exchange, and up-to-date information about legislation and new programs. Sample issues are available from Exceptional Parent, P.O. Box 3000, Dept. EP, Denville, NJ 07834.

Exceptional Parent also prints an Annual Directory of Organizations in one of its issues; this is also available from the above address for one dollar. It is a large, comprehensive directory that covers many organizations serving those with specific disorders that would ordinarily be difficult to find.

Family and Disability is a newsletter published by Beach Center on Families and Disability, Bureau of Child Research, 4138 Haworth Hall, Lawrence, KS 66045.

Clearinghouses, Information Networks, and Other Organizations

The March of Dimes Birth Defects Foundation has a wealth of informational materials. If there isn't an office in your local area, you may contact the national office at 1275 Mamaroneck Avenue, White Plains, NY 10605; phone 914-428-7100.

National Information Center for Children and Youth with Handicaps (NICHY). This federally funded clearinghouse and information center publishes *News Digest*, which is available at no cost. It provides information on virtually any topic regarding children's disabilities. P.O. Box 1492, Washington, DC 20013; phone 800-999-5599.

National Organization for Rare Disorders (NORD). This organization can link parents whose children have the same rare disorders. It also has developed the Rare Disease Database (RDB), which is available to people who subscribe to CompuServe (800-848-8199 for information). NORD also mails reprints of information requested to those who do not have computers. P.O. Box 8923, New Fairfield, CT; phone 203-746-6518.

Parent-to-Parent or Pilot Parents are local groups that provide helping parents to support families who have children born or newly diagnosed with a disability. Each group will operate under a local agency, and the agency will vary according to locality. To find a local group, call the local Association of Retarded Citizens, the United Way, or contact the Association for Retarded Citizens of the United States, 2501 Avenue J, Arlington, TX 76011; phone 800-433-5255 or 817-640-0204.

The Sibling Information Network. This is another clearinghouse of information, ideas, projects, literature, and research regarding siblings and other issues related to the needs of families with members who have disabilities. It publishes a quarterly newsletter, as well as a newsletter called *SIBAGE* (copies available) for children ages five through fifteen. Membership is five dollars annually for individuals and fifteen dollars for organizations. Connecticut's University Affiliated Program on Developmental Disabilities, 991 Main Street, East Hartford, CT 06108; phone 203-282-7050.

Special Olympics is an international organization that was created by the Joseph P. Kennedy, Jr. Foundation for citizens with mental retardation. Athletic training and competition in many sports is available on the local level, and competition takes place at local, state, national, and international events. Each state has a Special Olympics office. To find it, contact Special Olympics International, 1450 New York Avenue N.W., Washington, DC 20005; phone 202-628-3630.

These three information systems are housed in the Center for Developmental Disabilities, Benson Bldg., U. of South Carolina, Columbia, SC, 29208; 803-777-1435; Fax 803-777-6058. *National Information Clearinghouse,* for infants with disabilities and life-threatening conditions, offers a referral system for parents and professionals. Topics covered include medical, legal, financial, and parent education and support. Phone 800-922-9234; in South Carolina, 800-922-1107. *PSI-TECH* is for rehabilitation resources and assistive technology for those who require individual adaptation of environment or equipment. Phone 800-922-9234, ext. 301; in South Carolina, 800-922-1107, ext. 301. *NIS (National Information System)* for Vietnam veterans and families has counselors to assist those who have children with disabilities; provides assistance for genetic counseling and testing for and information on Agent Orange exposure. Phone 800-922-9234, ext. 401; in South Carolina, 800-922-1107, ext. 401.

Christian Organizations that Serve People with Disabilities

American Association on Mental Retardation, Religion Division; George G. Ducharme, president. 361 Granville Road, North Granby, CT 06060; phone 203-653-4166. Membership in the Religion Division of the AAMR is primarily at two levels—active and associate. There are journals, newsletters, and an annual convention. For a membershp brochure, call or write AAMR, 1719 Kalorama Road N.W., Washington, DC 20009; phone 800-424-3688.

5Faith and Light is an international ministry of L'Arche. There are 120 groups in the United States at present, and participants are usually members of Catholic churches. For information, contact the local diocesan Office for Persons with Disabilities, or a L'Arche home.

Joni and Friends, (Joni Eareckson Tada), P.O. Box 3333, Agoura Hills, CA 91301; phone 818-707-5664 or TDD No. 818-707-7006.

Logos Life and Light Foundation, Box 1732, Ormond Beach, FL 32175.

National Apostolate with Mentally Retarded Persons (NAMRP); Chuck Luce, executive director. P.O. Box 4711, Columbia, SC 29240; phone 803-782-2706 or 800-736-1280. NARMP is a Roman Catholic organization which helps persons who have mental retardation have an authentic participation in the life of the church; it also works to enhance the personal growth of those persons and to draw public attention to the spiritual, interpersonal, and other contributions persons who have mental retardation make to society. There are several levels of membership; all include a quarterly journal, and six newsletters a year.

National Catholic Office for Persons with Disabilities; Sister Rita Baum, SSJ, director. P.O. Box 29113, Washington, DC 20017; phone 202-529-2933 (this number also is for Voice/TDD).

Other State or Federal Resources

These vary by state; but some offices to search are:

Dept. of Special Education   Department of Social Services
Dept. of Rehabilitative Services   Department of Public Health
Dept. of Rights for the Disabled   Division of Vocational Rehabilitation

Parent Training and Information (PTI) Programs

This list of state PTI programs is from the Parent Educational Advocacy Training Center in Alexandria, Virginia:

Alabama

Carol Blades
Special Education Action Committee, Inc.
P.O. Box 161274
Mobile, AL 36616-2274
205-478-1208

Arizona

Mary Slaughter
Pilot Parents Inc.
2150 East Highland Avenue
Phoenix, AZ 85016
602-468-3001

Arkansas

Arkansas Parent Training Project

Bonnie Johnson
Arkansas Disability Coalition
10002 West Markham
Little Rock, AR 72205
501-221-1330

Barbara Semrau
FOCUS
2917 King Street,
Suite C
Jonesboro, AR 72401
501-935-2750

California

Joan Tellefson
TASK
18685 Santa Inez
Fountain Valley, CA 92708
714-962-6332

Florene Povadue
Parents Helping Parents
535 Race Street,
Suite 220
San Jose, CA 95126
408-288-5010

Pam Steneberg
DREDF
2212 6th Street
Berkeley, CA 94710
415-644-2555

Joan Kilburn
Disability Services Matrix
P.O. Box 6541
San Rafael, CA 94903
415-499-3877

Colorado

Judy Martz
Barbara Buswell
PEAK
6055 Lehman Drive, Suite 101
Colorado Springs, CO 80918
719-531-9400

Connecticut

Nancy Prescott
CT Parent Advocacy Center
P.O. Box 579
5 Church Lane, Suite #4
East Lyme, CT 06333
203-739-3089

Delaware

Marie-Ann Aghazadian
Executive Director
PIC of Delaware, Inc.
700 Barksdale Road, Suite 6
Newark, DE 19711
302-366-0152

Florida

Linda Pitts
Parent Education Network/Florida, Inc.
1211 Tech Boulevard, Suite 105
Tampa, FL 33619
813-623-4088

Georgia

Cheryl Knight
Parents Educating Parents (PEP)
Georgia ARC
1851 Ram Runway, Suite 104
College Park, GA 30337
404-761-2745

Don Bjornstad
Specialized Training of Military Parents
5004 Peachtree Street
Valdosta, GA 31602
912-244-4735

Hawaii

Ivalee Sinclair
Hawaii Association for Children and
    Adults with Learning Disabilities
200 North Vineyard Boulevard
Suite 103
Honolulu, HI 96817
808-536-9684

Idaho

Martha E. Gilgen
Idaho Parents Unlimited, Inc.
1365 North Orchard,
Suite #107
Boise, ID 83706
208-377-8049

Illinois

Charlotte Des Jardins
Coordinating Council for Handicapped Children
20 East Jackson Boulevard
Room 900
Chicago, IL 60604
312-939-3513

Donald Moore
Designs for Change
220 South State Street
Room 1900
Chicago, IL 60604
312-922-0317

Indiana

Richard Burden
Task Force on Education for the Handicapped, Inc.
833 Northside Boulevard, Building #1, rear
South Bend, IN 46617
219-234-7101

Iowa

Carla Lawson
Iowa Exceptional Parents Center
33 North 12th Street
P.O. Box 1151
Fort Dodge, IA 50501
515-576-5870

Kansas

Patricia Gerdel
Families Together, Inc.
3601 S.W. 29th St., #127
Topeka, KS 66614
(P.O. Box 86153, Topeka, KS 66686)
913-273-6343

Kentucky

Paulette Logsdon
Kentucky Special Parent Involvement Network
318 West Kentucky Street
Louisville, KY 40203
502-589-5717 or
502-584-1104

Louisiana

Sharon Duda
United Cerebral Palsy of Greater New Orleans
1500 Edwards Avenue, Suite O
Harahan, LA 70123
504-734-7736

Maine

Deborah Guimont
Special Needs Parent Information Network (SPIN)
P.O. Box 2067
Augusta, ME 04338
207-582-2504
800-325-0220 (in Maine only)

Massachusetts

Artie Higgins
Federation for Children with Special Needs
95 Berkeley Street,
Suite 104
Boston, MA 02116
617-482-2915
800-331-0688 (in Massachusetts only)

Michigan

Elmer L. Cerano
United Cerebral Palsy/
Detroit Community Service Department
17000 West 8 Mile Road, Suite 380
Southfield, MI 48075
313-557-5070

Cheryl Chilcote
Citizens Alliance to Uphold Special Education (CAUSE)
313 South Washington Square, lower level
Lansing, MI 48933
517-485-4084
800-221-9105 (in Michigan only)

Minnesota

Marge Goldberg
Paula F. Goldberg
PACER Center, Inc.
4826 Chicago Avenue South
Minneapolis, MN 55417
612-827-2966
800-53-PACER (in Minnesota only)
FAX 612-827-3065

Mississippi

Anne Presley
Association of Developmental Organizations of Mississippi
332 New Market Drive
Jackson, MS 39209
601-922-3210 or 800-231-3721

Missouri

Missouri Parents Act-MPACT
Marianne Toombs
1722-W South Glenstone, Suite 125
Springfield, MO 65804
417-882-7434

Pat Jones
625 Euclid, Room 225
St. Louis, MO 63108
314-361-1660

Montana

Katherine Kelker
Parents, Let's Unite for Kids, EMC/MCHC
1500 North 30th Street
Billings, MT 59101-0298
406-657-2055

Nebraska

Dan Costello
Nebraska Parent Information Training Center
3610 Dodge Street
Omaha, NE 68131
402-346-5220

New Hampshire

Judith Raskin
Parent Information Center
151A Manchester Street
P.O. Box 1422
Concord, NH 03302
603-224-6299, FAX 603-224-4365

New Jersey

Diana Cuthbertson, Executive Director
Statewide Parent Advocacy Network, Inc. (SPAN)
516 North Avenue East
Westfield, NJ 07090
201-654-7726

New Mexico

Norman Segel
EPICS Project
P.O. Box 788
2000 Camino del Pueblo
Bernalillo, NM 87004
505-867-3396

Linda Coleman
Stella Shaw-Petti
Project Adobe
1127 University N.E.
Albuquerque, NM 87102
505-842-9045

New York

Joan M. Watkins
Parent Network Center (PNC)
1443 Main Street
Buffalo, NY 14209
716-885-1004

Norma Rollins
Advocates for Children
New York City Org./Special Education
24-16 Bridge Plaza South
Long Island City, NY 11101
718-729-8866

North Carolina

Connie Hawkins
Exceptional Children's Assistance Center
P.O. Box 16
Davidson, NC 28036
704-892-1321

North Dakota

Katherine Erickson
Pathfinder Services of North Dakota
16th Street & 2nd Ave., S.W.
Arrowhead Shopping Center
Minot, ND 58701
701-268-3390

Ohio

Cathy Heizman
SOC Information Center
106 Wellington Place, Suite LL
Cincinnati, OH 45219
513-381-2400

Margaret Burley
Ohio Coalition for the Education of Handicapped Children
933 High Street, Suite 106
Worthington, OH 43085
614-431-1307

Oklahoma

Connie Motsinger
Parents Reaching Out in Oklahoma Project
1917 South Harvard Avenue
Oklahoma City, OK 73128
405-681-9710 or 800-PL9-4142

Oregon

Cheron Mayhall
Oregon COPE Project
999 Locust Street, N.E., Box B
Salem, OR 97303
503-373-7477 (Voice/TDD)

Pennsylvania

Christine Davis
Parents Union for Public Schools
2311 South Juniper Street, Suite 602
Philadelphia, PA 19107
215-546-1212

Gail Walker
Mentor Parent Program
Salina Road
P.O. Box 718
Seneca, PA 16346
814-676-8615
800-447-1431 (in Pennsylvania only)

Puerto Rico

Carmen Selles Vila
Asociacion de Padres
Pro Biene Star/Niños Impedidos de PR, Inc.
Box 21301
Rio Piedras, PR 00928
809-763-4665
765-0345

Tennessee

Dara Howe, Director
STEP
1805 Hayes Street, Suite 100
Nashville, TN 37203
615-327-0294

Texas

Janice Foreman
PATH
6465 Calder Avenue, Suite 202
Beaumont, TX 77707
409-866-4726

Utah

Helen W. Post
Utah PIC
2290 East 4500 South, Suite 110
Salt Lake City, UT 84117
801-272-1051
800-468-1160

Vermont

Joan Sylvester
Connie Curtin
VT Information and Training Network, Vermont/ARC
37 Champlain Mill
Winooski, VT 05404
802-655-4016

Virginia

Winifred Anderson
Parent Educational Advocacy Training Center
228 South Pitt Street, Room 300
Alexandria, VA 22314
703-836-2953

Washington

Martha Gentili
Washington PAVE
6316 South 12th Street
Tacoma, WA 98465
206-565-2266 (Voice/TDD)
800-5-PARENT

Heather Hebdon
PAVE/STOMP
Specialized Training of Military Parents
12208 Pacific Highway, S.W.
Tacoma, WA 98499
206-588-1741

Wisconsin

Liz Irwin
Parent Education Project
United Cerebral Palsy of Southeastern Wisconsin
230 West Wells Street
Suite 502
Milwaukee, WI 53203
414-272-4500

For Military Families

BABY (Birth and Beyond Years) is a support group which serves military families who have children with disabilities in San Diego, California. For information about this group, or information on forming a group in your area, call: Autovon, 735-7288; Commercial, 619-545-7288. Or, contact San Diego Armed Forces YMCA, 500 West Broadway, San Diego, CA 92101; phone 619-232-1133.

APPENDIX III
TRUSTS FOR THOSE WITH DISABILITIES

Kent County Sentry Fund
1331 Lake Drive, SE
Grand Rapids, MI 49506
616-459-3339

Planned Lifetime Assistance Network (PLAN)
P.O. Box 323
Charlottesville, VA 22902
804-977-9002

Maryland Trust for Retarded Citizens
180 Krider's Church Road
Westminster, MD 21157
301-876-1836

Virginia Beach Community Trust for Developmentally Disabled Individuals
Community Services Board
MR/DD Programs
Pembroke Six, Suite 218
Virginia Beach, VA 23462
804-473-5223

New York Trust for Retarded Individuals
New York State Association for Retarded Citizens
393 Delaware Avenue
Delmar, NY 12054
518-439-8311

Gallant and Gallant
850 Grand Avenue
New Haven, CT 06511
203-624-2184

TARCARE Beneficiary Trust
TARC Guardianship Program
ARC-Topeka
2701 Randolph
Topeka, KS 66611
913-232-0597

PLAN NJ (Planned Lifetime Assistance Network of New Jersey)
985 Livingston Ave.
North Brunswick, NJ 08902

ComTrust (a trust program for handicapped citizens in Tennessee)
Comcare, Inc.
P.O. Box 1885
Greenville, TN 37744
615-638-3926

These trusts are current as of September, 1990. Interested individuals may wish to contact their local or state office of the Association for Retarded Citizens or State Developmental Disability Office for further information.

L'ARCHE HOMES AND CAMPHILL VILLAGES

L'Arche Homes

AUSTRALIA

L'Arche Sydney
306 Burwood Road
Burwood 2134, NSW
Tel: (2) 747 53 16

Beni Abbes
40 Pirie Street
Tasmania
New Town 7008
Tel: (002) 28 31 68

Genesaret
PO Box 1326
Woden, ACT 2606
Tel: 81 26 30 (H)
        82 27 27 (O)

BELGIUM

Aquero
14 rue St Pierre
B-1301 Bièrges
Tel: (10) 41 43 86

Ark Antwerpen
Madona
12 Janssenlei
B-2530 Boechout
Tel: (3) 455 4532

L'Arche Bruxelles
35 rue des Bataves
B-1040 Bruxelles
Tel: (2) 734 3623

Le Murmure
49 rue du Châlet
4070 Aywaille
Tel: 41 84 64 84

L'Arche Namur
Chaussée de Waterloo 118
B-5002 St. Servais
Tel: 81 73 02 83
            (Cascatelle)
        81 21 41 60 (Bartrès)

BRAZIL

L'Arche°
Arca do Brasil
R. Manuel Aquilino dos
Santos, 151
JD Elisa Maria CEP 02873
Sao Paulo - Sp.1
Tel: (011) 8585622

BURKINA FASO

Nongr Maasem
BP 1492
Ouagadougou
Burkina Faso
Tel: 226 31 04 35

CANADA

L'Arche Agapé
19, rue Front
Hull, Quebec
J8Y 3M4
Tel: (819) 770-2000 (O)

Alleluia House
9 Melrose Avenue
Ottawa, Ontario
K1Y 1T8
Tel: (613) 729 1601

L'Arche Antigonish
69 St. Ninian Street
Antigonish, Nova Scotia
B2G 1Y7
Tel: (902) 863 5945

Arc-en-Ciel
1570 30e Rue
St. Prosper
Beauce, Quebec G0M 1Y0
Tel: (418) 594 5604

L'Arche Calgary
429 54th Ave. S.W.
Calgary, Alberta
T2V 0C6
Tel: (403) 255 3909 (O)
       (403) 255 4728 (H)

La Caravane
R.R.2
Green Valley, Ontario
K0C 1L0
Tel: (613) 525 1921 (O)

L'Arche Cape Breton
R.R.1
Orangedale, Nova Scotia
B0E 2K0
Tel: (902) 756 2976

Daybreak
11339 Yonge Street
Richmond Hill, Ontario
L4C 4X7
Tel: (416) 884 3454

Emmaus House
1241 Parisien Street
Sudbury, Ontario
P3A 3B5
Tel: (705) 560 1966

L'Etable
2663 Fernwood Ave.
Victoria, British Colombia
V8T 3A1
Tel: (604) 595 1014

L'Etoile
617 Franklin
Quebec
G1N 2I7
Tel: (418) 648 9588 (O)
       (418) 681 9446 (H)

Fleurs de Soleil
221 Bernard Pilon
Beloeil P.Q.
J3G 1V2
Tel: (514) 467 9655

L'Arche Arnprior
23 Lake Street
Arnprior, Ontario
K7S 1Z9
Tel: (613) 623 7323 (O)
       (613) 623 0129 (H)

L'Arche Hamilton
78 Sherman Ave. S.
Hamilton, Ontario
L8M 2P7
Tel: (416) 544 5401

Homefires
PO Box 1296
Wolfville, Nova Scotia
B0P 1X0
Tel: (902) 542 3520

Kara Foyer
102 First Ave. East
North Bay, Ontario
P1B 1J6
Tel: (705) 474 0168

La Maison de l'Amitié°
239 Des Erables
Cap de la Madeleine
Quebec
G8T 5G9
Tel: (819) 375 2790

Le Printemps
100 route Frampton
St. Malachie, Quebec
G0R 3N0
Tel: (418) 642 5785 (O)
       (418) 642 5000
       (maison Gaston)

Le Saule Fragile°
191 2nd Avenue West
Amos, Quebec
J9T 1S4
Tel: (819) 732 5036

Maranatha
82 Huron Street
Stratford, Ontario
N5A 5S6
Tel: (519) 271 9751

Shalom
7708-83 Street
Edmonton, Alberta
T6C 2Y8
Tel: (403) 465 0618

Shiloah
7401 Sussex Avenue
Burnaby, British Columbia
V5J 3V6
Tel: (604) 434 1933 (O)
       (604) 435 9544 (H)

The Skiff
1030 3e Avenue
Verdun, P.Q.
H4G 2X8
Tel: (514) 761 7270

L'Arche Winnipeg
128 Victoria Avenue West
Winnipeg, Manitoba
R2C 1S5
Tel: (204) 224 2692
       (204) 224 2626

DENMARK

Niels Steensens Hus
Nygade 6
3000 Helsingor
Tel: (2) 21 21 39

**DOMINICAN
REPUBLIC**

Comunidad del Arca
Apdo. 1104
Santo Domingo
Tel: (809) 547 3543

FRANCE

Aigrefoin
78470 St. Rémy les
Chevreuses
Tel: (1) 30 52 21 07

L'Arc-en-ciel
11 rue François Mouthon
75015 Paris
Tel: (1) 45 32 83 91 (H)
       (1) 42 50 06 48 (O)

L'Arche
BP 35
Trosly-Breuil
60350 Cuise-la-Motte
Tel: (1) 44 85 61 02

L'Atre
21 rue Obert
59118 Wambrechies
Tel: 20 78 81 52

Communauté de l'Arche
Ecorcheboeuf
76590 Anneville-sur-Scie
Tel: 35 04 40 31

Le Caillou Blanc°
La Fabrique
Clohars Fouesnant
29118 Bénodet
Tel: 98 54 60 05

Le Levain
1 Place St. Clément
60200 Compiègno
Tel: 44 86 25 03

La Merci
Courbillac
16200 Jarnac
Tel: 45 21 74 16

Moita
St. Germain
26390 Hauterives
Tel: 75 68 81 84

L'Olivier°
30 rue de la Noé
35170 Bruz
Tel: 99 52 72 74

La Rebellerie
49560 Nueil-sur-Layon
Tel: 41 59 58 79

La Ruisselée°
72220 St. Mars d'Oudllé
Tel: 43 42 76 66

Les Sapins°
Les Abels
Lignières-Sonneville
16130 Segonzac
Tel: 45 80 50 66

Le Sénevé°
21 rue l'Abbé Larose
44190 Gorges
Tel: 40 06 96 23

La Vigne°
5 rue Brillat Savarin
21000 Dijon
Tel: 80 66 12 37

GERMANY

Arche Regenbogen°
Apfelallee 23
4542 Tecklenburg
Tel: (49) 54 82 77 00

Arche Volksdorf°
Farmsener Landstr. 198
D-2000 Hamburg 67
Tel: 040 603 71 22

HAITI

L'Arche de Carrefour
BP 11075
Carrefour
Port-au-Prince
Haiti
Tel: 509 14 42 55

L'Arche Chantal
Zone des Cayes
CP 63 Cayes
Haiti

HONDURAS

El Arca de Honduras
Apartado 1273
Tegucigalpa DF
Tel: 504 32 77 92

Comunidad del Arca°
Casa san José
Apartado 241
Choluteca

INDIA

Asha Niketan
53/7 Bannerghatta Rd.
Bangalore 560029
India
Tel: (81) 64 03 49

Asha Niketan
37 Tangra Road
(Pulin Khatichs)
Calcutta 700009
Tel: (33) 35 6299

Asha Niketan
Nandi Bazaar P.O.
Katalur
Calicut DT
Kerala 673531
India

Asha Niketan
Kottivakkam
Tiruvanmiyur P.O.
Madras 600041
India
Tel: (44) 41 6298

IRELAND

L'Arche Cork
Green Park, Wilton Lawn
Wilton, Cork
Ireland
Tel: 353 (21) 34 26 16

Moorfield House
Kilmoganny
Co. Kilkenny
Ireland
Tel: 353 (56) 256 28

ITALY

Il Chicco
Via Ancona 1
00043 Ciampino
Roma
Tel: (39) 6 617 11 34 (H)
       (39) 6 727 21 04 (O)

IVORY COAST

L'Arche de Bouaké
04 BP 373
Bouaké 04
République de Côte d'Ivoire
Tel: 225 63 44 53

MEXICO

Comunidad del Arca°
Apartado Postale 55-232
Mexico DF 09000
Tel: (52) 855 64 57

PHILIPPINES

Ang Arko 'Punla'
307 D. Valencia Street
Nagtahan Sampaloc
Metro Manila
Tel: (63) 2 609 435

POLAND

Arka
Sledziejowice 83
32020 Wielizka

SPAIN

El Rusc
Lista de Correos
Tordera
Barcelona 008399
Tel: (93) 764 0150 (El
Rusc)
          (93) 83 00 301 (Moia)

Els Avets°
08180 Moia
Tel: (93) 83 00 301

SWITZERLAND

Im Nauen°
Kirchgasse
4146 Hochwald
Tel: 061 78 4933

La Corolle
26 Chemin d'Ecogia
1290 Versoix
Geneva
Tel: 41 (22) 55 5189

UNITED STATES

The Arch
402 South 4th Street
Clinton, IA 52732
Tel: (319) 243 3980 (H)
          (319) 243 9035 (O)

L'Arche Syracuse
1701 James Street
Syracuse, NY 13206
Tel: (315) 437 9337 (O)
          (315) 471 5862 (H)

Community of the Ark
2474 Ontario Road N.W.
Washington, DC 20009
Tel: (202) 462 3924

The Hearth
523 West 8th Street
Erie, PA 16502
Tel: (814) 459 4850 (H)
          (814) 452 2065 (O)

Hope
151 S. Ann St.
Mobile, AL 36604
Tel: (205) 438 6738 (H)
          (205) 438 2094 (O)

Irenicon
73 Lamoille Avenue
Havenhill, MA 01830
Tel: (508) 374 6928 (O)
          (508) 374 9162 (H)

Lamb of God
1730 E. 70th Street
Cleveland, OH 44103
Tel: (216) 881 0682 (H)
          (216) 881 7015 (O)

L'Arche°
9187 West 85th St.
Overland Park
Kansas, MO 66212
Tel: (913) 642 6070

Noah Sealth
816 15th Avenue East
Seattle, WA 98112
Tel: (206) 325 8912

Spokane Nazareth
E 3403 Farwell Road
Mead, WA 99021
Tel: (509) 466 9713

Tahoma Hope
The Farmhouse
11716 Vickery Road East
Tacoma, WA 98446
Tel: (206) 535 3171 (H)
          (206) 535 3178 (O)

UNITED KINGDOM

L'Arche Liverpool
'The Ark Workshops'
Lockerby Road
Liverpool L7 0HG
Tel: 051-260-4022
          051-260-3080

L'Arche Bognor Regis
Emmaus
123 Longford Road
Bognor Regis
West Sussex PO21 1AE
England
Tel: (243) 86 3426 (O)

L'Arche Brecon
Corlan y Bryn°
120 Cradoc Close
Brecon
Powys, Wales
Tel: 0874 4950

L'Arche Inverness
Braerannoch
13 Drummond Crescent
Inverness
Scotland
Tel: (463) 23 9615 (O)
          (463) 23 8921 (H)

L'Arche Kent
Little Ewell
Barfrestone, Dover
Kent CT15 7JJ
England
Tel: (304) 83 0930 (O)
          (304) 83 1090 (H)

Lambeth l'Arche
15 Norwood High Street
West Norwood
London SE27
England
Tel: (81) 670 6714 (O)

WEST BANK

Beit-al-Rafiq°
B.P. 51214
Jerusalem
Israel

°Probationary member

Camphill Villages

Camphill Special Schools
Beaver Run
R.D. 1
Glenmoore, PA 19343
215-469-9236
A children's village and
school community for
children with mental
disabilities.

Camphill Village Kimberton
Hills
P.O. Box 155
Kimberton, PA 19442
215-935-0300
An agricultural community
with adults who have mental
disabilities.

Camphill Village U.S.A., INC.
Copake, NY 12516
518-329-4851
A community with adults
who have mental disabilities.

Triform Enterprises,
Limited
R.D. 4, Box 151
Hudson, N.Y. 12534
518-851-9320
A training and apprentice-
ship community with special
adults.

Camphill Village Minnesota
Pughtown Road
Route 3, Box 249
Sauk Centre, MN 56378
612-732-6365
A rural community with
adults who have mental
disabilities.

Camphill Foundation
Pughtown Road
P.O. Box 290
Kimberton, PA 19442
215-935-0200

Camphill Village Ontario
Rural Route #1
Angus, Ontario, Canada
L0M-1B0

704-424-5363

To apply to be a part of a Camphill adult community, send a short life history addressed to the Admissions Group, listing interests, skills, and questions. When the application is for a person with a disability who is over eighteen, medical and psychological reports are also requested. The Admissions Group will review the application, and arrange for an interview and a trial period. All newcomers are encouraged to visit for at least one month, so that the decision to join the community is a mutual one between both the individual and the community.

NOTES

Chapter 1. An Overview of Disability

1. *Pacesetter* newsletter (Minneapolis, Minn.: The PACER Center, September 1989):13.

2. "People First Language," *Focal Point* 3 (1989):12.

3. *Webster's New Collegiate Dictionary*, (G. & C. Merriam Co., 1981).

4. *Diagnostic and Statistical Manual of Mental Disorders*, 3d ed., rev. [*DSM-III-R*] (Washington, D.C.: American Psychiatric Association, 1987).

5. Vicky Lewis, *Development and Handicap* (New York: Basil Blackwell Ltd., 1987), 3.

6. *DSM–III–R*, 27–95.

7. Ibid., 49–58.

8. Kathleen Burch Caries and Marie Weil, "Developmentally Disabled Persons and Their Families," in Marie Weil, James M. Karls, and Associates, eds., *Case Management in Human Services* (San Francisco: Jossey-Bass, 1985), 234.

9. John L. Czajka, *Digest of Data on Persons with Disabilities*. A report prepared for the Office of Special Education and Rehabilitative Services, Washington, D.C., 1984, xiii.

10. Ibid.

11. Ibid., 24.

12. Ibid., 48.

13. Ibid., 13.

14. *The Truth About Mental Retardation* (Arlington, Tex.: Association for Retarded Citizens), 3.

15. *DSM–III–R*, 31.

16. *The Truth About Mental Retardation*, 3.

17. Cornelius M. Pietzner, ed., *Village Life* (Natick, Mass.: Alphabet Press, 1986).

18. George Harris, "L'Arche: Homes for People Who Are Mentally Retarded," *Journal of Counseling and Development* 65 (1987):322–24.

19. The Center for Education in Human Genetics, *Basic Genetics, A Human Approach* (Colorado Springs: BSCS, 1983), 3.

20. U.S. Bureau of the Census, *Statistical Abstract of the United States,* 109th ed. (Washington, D.C.: 1989), Table 233.

21. Mark L. Batshaw and Yvonne M. Perret, *Children with Handicaps* 2d. ed., (Baltimore: Paul H. Brookes, 1986).

22. *DSM–III–R*, 32.

23. Ibid.

24. Ibid., 33.

25. Ibid.

Chapter 2. The Five-Factor Model of Family Stress and Crisis

1. Robert Byrne, *1,911 Best Things Anybody Ever Said* (New York: Fawertt-Columbine, 1988), 11.

2. Helen Mederer and Reuben Hill, "Critical Transitions over the Family Life Span: Theory and Research," in Hamilton I. McCubbin, Marvin B. Sussman, and Joan M. Patterson, eds., *Social Stress and the Family* (New York: Haworth Press, 1983), 40–41.

3. Burt E. Gilliland and Richard K. James, *Crisis Intervention Strategies* (Pacific Grove, Calif.: Brooks/Cole, 1988), 3.

4. Robert D. Felner, Richard T. Rowlison, and Lisa Terre, "Unraveling the Gordian Knot in Life Change Inquiry," in Stephen M. Auerbach and Arnold L. Stolber, eds., *Crisis Intervention with Children and Families* (Washington, D.C.: Hemisphere, 1986), 41.

5. Ibid.

6. Ibid.

7. Ibid.

8. Ibid., 42.

9. Ibid.

10. Ibid.

11. Lydia Rapoport, "The State of Crisis: Some Theoretical Considerations," in Howard J. Parad, ed. *Crisis Intervention: Selected Readings* (New York: Family Service Association of America, 1965), 26.

12. Gilliland and James, *Crisis Intervention Strategies*, 4.

13. Rapoport, "The State of Crisis," 23.

14. Ibid., 25.

15. E. H. Janosik and Ellen Hastings, *Crisis Counseling: A Contemporary Approach* (Monterey, Calif.: Wadsworth, 1984), 39.

16. Mederer and Hill, "Critical Transitions," 49.

17. Ibid., 50.

18. David M. Klein and Reuben Hill, "Determinants of Family Problems-Solving Effectiveness," in Wesley R. Burr, Reuben Hill, F. Ivan Nye, and Ira L. Reiss, eds., *Contemporary Theories About the Family*, vol. I (New York: The Free Press, 1979), 510–27.

19. T. Holmes and R. Rahe, "The Scale," *Journal of Psychosomatic Research* II (1967):213–18.

20. Felner, Rowlison, and Terre, "Unraveling the Gordian Knot," 46–47.

21. Ibid.

22. Ibid.

23. Ibid., 48–49.

24. Ibid.

25. *Webster's New Collegiate Dictionary*.

26. Reuben Hill, *Families Under Stress* (New York: Harper and Row, 1949).

27. Everett L. Worthington, Jr., *Counseling for Unplanned Pregnancy and Infertility*, vol. 10 of the Resources for Christian Counseling Series (Waco, Tex.: Word, 1987), 39–44.

28. Steven D. Brown and Linda Heath, "Coping with Critical Life Events: An Integrative Cognitive-Behavioral Model for Research and Practice," in Steven D. Brown and Robert W. Lent, eds., *Handbook of Counseling Psychology* (New York: John Wiley and Sons, 1984).

29. Reuben Hill, "Generic Features of Families Under Stress," in Howard J Parad, ed., *Crisis Intervention: Selected Readings* (New

York: Family Services Association of America, 1965), 36. (Please note that Hill makes no mention of faith in his model. That has been added by this author.)

30. Ibid. 41–43.

31. Ibid. 43–44.

32. Hamilton I. McCubbin and Joan M. Patterson, "Family Adaptations to Crises," in Hamilton I. McCubbin, A. Elizabeth Cauble, and Joan M. Patterson, eds., *Family Stress, Coping and Social Support* (Springfield, Ill.: Charles C. Thomas, 1982), 39.

33. Ibid., 43.

34. Rapoport, "The State of Crisis: Some Theoretical Considerations," in Howard J. Parad, ed., *Crisis Intervention: Selected Readings* (New York: Family Service Association of America, 1965), 25.

35. Steven D. Brown and Linda Heath, "Coping with Critical Life Events," 548.

36. Gerard Egan, *The Skilled Helper: A Systematic Approach to Effective Helping*, 4th ed. (Pacific Grove, Calif.: Brooks/Cole, 1990), 153.

37. J. Dale Munro, "Counseling Severely Dysfunctional Families of Mentally and Physically Disabled Persons," *Clinical Social Work Journal* 13 (1985):18–32.

38. Ibid.

Chapter 3. Prenatal and Postnatal Diagnoses

1. Siegfried M. Pueschel, James C. Bernier, and Leslie E. Weidenmen, *The Special Child* (Baltimore: Paul H. Brookes, 1988), 169.

2. Lew Lord, Douglas Stanglin, et al., "Sonograms Are Eye Openers," *U.S. News and World Report* 105 (3 October 1989):10.

3. Mark L. Batshaw and Yvonne M. Perret, *Children with Handicaps*, 2d ed. (Baltimore: Paul H. Brookes, 1986), 30.

4. Pueschel, Bernier, and Weidenmen, *The Special Child,* 169.

5. Phone conversation, Dr. George Knight, Foundation for Blood Research, Scarborough, Maine, 7 December 1989.

6. Phone conversation, Dr. Diana W. Bianchi, The Boston Children's Hospital, 7 December 1989.

7. Gina Kolata, "Fetal Therapy, A Question of Ethics," *The Virginian-Pilot and the Ledger-Star,* 16 June 1989, C1, C3.

8. Ibid.

9. Ibid.

10. A helpful resource may be *Resources for Clergy in Human Genetic Problems*, 2d ed. (Washington, D.C.: National Center for Education in Maternal and Child Health, 1988). See Appendix II for information on how to order.

11. Pueschel, Bernier, and Weidenman, *The Special Child*, 171–73.

12. "Style Roundup" column, *The Pittsburgh Press*, 25 June 1989, J3.

13. Phillip Elmer-DeWitt, "The Perils of Treading on Heredity," *Time*, 20 March 1989, 70–71.

14. Kenneth W. Dumars, Deborah Duran-Flores, Carol Foster, and Stanley Stills, "Screening Developmental Disabilities," in Helen M. Wallace, Robert F. Biehl, Lawrence Taft, Allan C. Oglesby, eds., *Handicapped Children and Youth* (New York: Human Sciences Press), 115.

15. The discussion on chromosomes is from Pueschel, Bernier, and Weidenman, *The Special Child*, 91–101.

16. Mark L. Batshaw and Yvonne M Perret, *Children with Handicaps*, 2d ed. (Baltimore: Paul H. Brookes, 1986), 408.

17. Georgiana M. Jagiello, Jye-Siung Fang, Mercedes B. Ducayen, and Wang Kong Sung. "Etiology of Human Trisomy 21," in Siegfried M. Pueschel, Carol Tingey, John E. Rynders, Allen C. Crocker, and Diane M. Crutcher, eds., *New Perspectives on Down Syndrome* (Baltimore: Paul H. Brookes, 1987).

18. Allan Sieffert, "Parents' Initial Reactions to Having a Mentally Retarded Child: A Concept and Model for Social Workers," *Clinical Social Work Journal* 6 (1978):33–43.

19. Anne M. Bauer and Thomas M. Shea, "An Integrative Perspective on Adaptation to the Birth or Diagnosis of an Exceptional Child," *Social Work in Education* (Summer 1987):240–52.

20. Sieffert, "Parents' Initial Reactions," 42.

21. Marianne Spain Kratochvil and Sally Ann Devereux, "Counseling Needs of Parents of Handicapped Children," *Social Casework* 69 (1988):420–26.

22. Simon Olshansky, "Chronic Sorrow: A Response to Having a Mentally Defective Child," *Social Casework* 43 (1962):190–94.

23. Robert H. Schuller, *Tough Minded Faith for Tender Hearted People* (Nashville: Thomas Nelson Publishers, 1983):123.

24. Jan Blacher, "A dynamic perspective on the impact of a severely handicapped child in the family," in Jan Blacher, ed., *Severely Handicapped Young Children and Their Families* (Orlando, Fla.: Academic Press, 1984), 3–50.

25. S. Cino and F. G. Caro, *Supporting Families Who Care for Severely Disabled Children at Home: A Public Policy Perspective.* A report prepared for the Community Services Society of New York, 1984.

Chapter 4. The Toddler/Preschool Years

1. James J. Gallagher, Paula Beckman, and Arthur H. Cross. "Families of Handicapped Children: Sources of Stress and Its Amelioration," *Exceptional Children* 50 (1983):10–19

2. Linda K. Girdner and Brenda Krause Eheart, "Mediation with Families Having a Handicapped Child," *Family Relations* 33 (1984):187–94.

3. Elizabeth Gordon, *Living with a Handicapped Child: The Impact on the Family. A Literature Review* (ERIC Document ED 203–557, September 1980):24.

4. S. T. Cummings, et al., "Effects of the Child's Deficiency on the Mother: A Study of Mothers of Mentally Retarded, Chronically Ill and Neurotic Children," *American Journal of Orthopsychology* 36 (1966):595–605; and W. H. Ehlers, *Mothers of Retarded Children: How They Feel* (Springfield, Ill.: Charles C. Thomas, 1966).

5. Milton Seligman, "Handicapped Children and Their Families," *Journal of Counseling and Development* 64 (1985):274–77.

6. A bibliography from the Sibling Information Network (see Appendix II) of January 1988 lists over one hundred journal articles, books, and dissertations that deal with siblings of children with disabilities. Also see D. J. Mayer, P. F. Vadasy, and R. R. Fewell, *Living with a Brother or Sister with Special Needs: A Book for Siblings* (Seattle: University of Washington Press, 1985).

7. P. K. Mölsä and S. A. Ikonen-Mölsä, "The Mentally Handicapped Child and Family Crisis," *Journal of Mental Deficiency Research* 29 (1985):309–14; and I. M. Sonnek, "Grandparents and the Extended Family," in Rebecca R. Fewell and Patricia F. Vadasy, ed., *Families of Handicapped Children* (Austin, Tex.: Pro-Ed, 1986).

8. E. A. Byrne and C. C. Cunningham, "The Effects of Mentally Handicapped Children on Families—A Conceptual Review," *Journal of Child Psychology and Psychiatry* 26 (1985):847–64.

9. Rebecca R. Fewell and Patricia F. Vadasy, eds., *Families of Handicapped Children* (Austin, Tex.: Pro-Ed, 1986); Jan Blacker, ed., *Severely Handicapped Young Children and Their Families* (Orlando,

Fla.: Academic Press, 1984); and Milton Seligman and Rosalyn Benjamin Darling, *Ordinary Families, Special Children: A Systems Approach to Childhood Disability* (New York: Guilford Press, 1989).

10. Linda K. Girdner and Brenda Krause Earheart, "Mediation with Families," 187.

11. Ibid., 189.

12. Ibid.

13. Fern Kupfer, *Before and After Zachariah* (New York: Delacorte Press, 1982), 8.

14. Marianne Spain Kratochvil and Sally Ann Devereaux, "Counseling Needs of Parents of Handicapped Children," *Social Casework* 69 (1988):420–26.

15. Margaret Roberts, "Three Mothers: Life Span Experiences," in Rebecca R. Fewell and Patricia F. Vadasy, eds., *Families of Handicapped Children* (Austin, Tex.: Pro-Ed, 1986), 198.

16. Ibid., 199.

17. Ibid., 203.

Chapter 5. The School Years

1. Victoria D. Weisfeld, ed., *Serving Handicapped Children, A Special Report* (Princeton, N.J.: The Robert Wood Johnson Foundation, 1988), 3–4, 8–9.

2. Anne E. Kazak, "Families with Disabled Children: Stress and Social Networks in Three Samples," *Journal of Abnormal Child Psychology* 15 (1987):137–46.

3. Bruce L. Mallory, "Community Agencies and Families Over the Life Cycle," in Rebecca R. Fewell and Patricia F. Vadasy, eds., *Families of Handicapped Children* (Austin, Tex.: Pro-Ed Inc., 1986).

4. Ibid., 326.

5. Winifred Anderson, Stephen Chitwood, and Deidre Hayden, *Negotiating the Special Education Maze*, 2d ed. (Englewood Cliffs, N.J.: Prentice-Hall, 1990), 208–10.

6. Ibid., 6, 8.

7. Allen E. Ivey, *International Interviewing and Counseling*, 2d ed. (Pacific Grove, Calif.: Brooks/Cole, 1988), 85.

8. Ibid., 183.

9. Ibid., 184.

10. Ibid.

11. Ibid., 186.

12. Ibid.

13. Betty Pendler, "Parents Are Like Tea Bags," *Exceptional Parent* 20 (1990):56.

Chapter 6. Transitioning: The School Bus Isn't Coming Any More

1. "All Things Considered," National Public Radio, 20 February 1990.

2. "Community Interaction for Virginians with Developmental Disabilities," a summary of recommendations from a conference held by the Virginia Institute for Developmental Disabilities, Virginia Commonwealth University, Richmond, Va., (15–16 September 1986):23–27, 38, 40–41.

3. Ed Blazina, "Experimental Consortiums Run Group Homes in Ohio," *The Pittsburgh Press*, 26 June 1989.

4. Ed Blazina, "Falling-Apart Systems Abandoning Retarded Adults," *The Pittsburgh Press*, 25 June 1989.

5. Paul Retish, William Hitchings, and Stephanie Hitchings, "Parents' Perspective of Vocational Services for Moderately Retarded Individuals," *Journal of Career Development* 13 (1987):52–62.

6. S. Wayne Mulkey and Connie C. Brechin, "Transition-to-Work: The Physical Pursuit," *Journal of Rehabilitation* 54 (1988):31–36.

7. Janet Hill, et al., "Parents' Attitudes About Working Conditions of Their Mentally Retarded Sons and Daughters," *Exceptional Children* 54 (1987):9–23.

8. Patrick J. Schloss, Constance W. Wolf, and Cynthia N. Schloss, "Financial Implications of Half- and Full-Time Employment for Persons with Disabilities," *Exceptional Children* 54 (1987):272–76.

9. Anne E. Kazak, "Families with Disabled Children: Stress and Social Networks in Three Samples," *Journal of Abnormal Children*, 15 (1987):137–46.

10. H. Norman Wright, *Crisis Counseling: Helping People in Crisis and Stress* (San Bernardino, Calif.: Here's Life Publishers, 1985):180.

11. James C. Chalfant, "Diagnostic Criteria for Entry and Exit from Service," in Larry B. Siver, ed., *The Assessment of Learning Disabilities* (Boston, Mass.: Little-Brown Co., 1989).

12. Margaretha Vreeburg Izzo, "Career Development of Disabled Youth," *Journal of Career Development* 13 (1987):47–55.

13. H. Norman Wright, *Crisis Counseling*, 190–91.

14. Lynn Wikler, Mona Wason, and Elaine Hatfield, "Seeking Strengths in Families of Developmentally Disabled Children," *Social Work* 28 (1983):313–15.

15. Ibid., 314.

16. T. H. Powell and P. A. Ogle, *Brothers and Sisters: A Special Part of Exceptional Families* (Baltimore: Paul H. Brookes, 1985). Cited in *NICHY News Digest* 11 (1988):1.

17. Linda K. Girdner and Brenda Krause Earheart, "Mediation with Families Having a Handicapped Child," *Family Relations* 33 (1984):189–94.

18. Ibid., 190.

19. Frank R. Rusch and L. Allen Phelps, "Secondary Special Education and Transition form School to Work: A National Priority," *Exceptional Children* 53 (1987):487–92.

Chapter 7. Providing for the Future

1. "From the Bookshelf," *Exceptional Parent* (1984):45–46.

2. U. S. Bureau of the Census, *Statistical Abstract of the United States,* 108th ed., (Washington, D.C., 1988). Table 106.

3. Ibid., Table 16.

4. Edward E. Marcus and Robert J. Havighurst, "Education for the Aging," in Edgar J. Boone, Ronald W. Shearer, Estelle E. White, and Associates, eds., *Serving Personal and Community Needs Through Adult Education* (San Francisco: Jossey-Bass, 1980).

5. Vivian McCoy, "Adult Life Cycle Changes," *Lifelong Learning: The Adult Years* (October 1977):14ff.

6. Michael Hurst, "Young Adults with Disabilities: Health, Employment and Financial Costs for Family Careers," *Child Care, Health and Development* 11 (1985):291–307.

7. Anne E. Kazak, "Stress and Social Networks in Families with Older Institutionalized Retarded Children," *Journal of Social and Clinical Psychology* 6 (1988):448–61.

8. Lesley Winik, Andrea G. Zetlin, and Sandra Z. Kaufman, "Adult Mildly Retarded Persons and Their Parents: The Relationship Between Involvement and Adjustment," *Applied Research in Mental Retardation* 6 (1985):409–19.

9. Jean L. Engelhardt, Victoria D. Lutzer, and Timothy H. Brubaker, "Parents of Adults with Developmental Disabilities: Age

and Reasons for Reluctance to Use Another Caregiver," *Lifestyles* 8 (1987):47–54.

10. Steven Stone, "Man Wounded by Mother Was Model Worker," *The Virginian-Pilot and the Ledger-Star,* 4 March 1990.

11. Marsha Mailick Seltzer, Marty Wyngaarden Krauss, and Leon C. Litchfield, *Aging Parents with Mentally Retarded Children: The Impact of Lifelong Caregiving* (Boston: Boston University, School of Social Work, 1989). A report submitted to the American Association of Retired Persons (AARP) Andrus Foundation, Washington, D.C., pp. 71–72.

12. M. M. Bristol, J. J. Gallagher, and E. Schopler, *Developmental Psychology* (1988) 24:441–51, cited in report noted in n. 11 above.

13. Denise M. Topolnicki, "Protecting the Future of a Child Who's Handicapped," *Money* (November 1988):94–102.

14. James R. Dudley, "Speaking for Themselves: People Who Are Labeled as Mentally Retarded," *Social Work* (January-February 1987):80–82.

15. Carol Tingey, "Cutting the Umbilical Cord," in Sigfreid M. Pueschel, ed., *The Young Person with Down Syndrome* (Baltimore: Paul H. Brookes, 1988).

16. Jean Vanier, *Community and Growth* (New York: Paulist Press, 1979), xi.

17. Cornelius M. Pietzner, ed., *Village Life,* (Natick, Mass.: Alphabet Press, 1986).

18. Christine Rinck, Jane Berg, and Carol Hafeman, "The Adolescent with Meyelomeninogocele: A Review of Parent Experiences and Expectations," *Adolescence* 24 (1989):699–710.

19. George Harris, "L'Arche: Homes for People Who Are Mentally Retarded," *Journal of Counseling and Development* 65 (1987):322–24.

20. Reed Greenwood, "Expanding Community Participation by People with Disabilities: Implications for Counselors," *Journal of Counseling and Development* 66 (1987):185–87.

21. Jerelyn B. Schultz and Donna U. Adams, "Family Life Education Needs of Mentally Disabled Adolescents, *Adolescence* 22 (1987):221–30.

22. Paul R. Abramson, Tracee Parker and Sheila Weisberg, "Sexual Expression of Mentally Retarded People: Educational and Legal Implications," *American Journal on Mental Retardation* 93 (1988):328–34.

23. Jean Vanier, *Man and Woman He Made Them* (Mahwah, N.J.: Paulist Press, 1985).

24. Carol Tingey, "Cutting the Umbilical Cord," 19–20.

Chapter 8. Effects on the Marital Couple and the Siblings

1. Anne E. Kazak and Robert S. Marvin, "Differences, Difficulties, and Adaptation: Stress and Social Networks in Families with a Handicapped Child," *Family Relations* 33 (1984):67–77.

2. Dianne C. Longo and Linda Bond, "Families of the Handicapped Child: Research and Practice," *Families Relations* 33 (1984):57–65.

3. Kazak and Marvin, "Differences, Difficulties, and Adaptation," 68.

4. Longo and Bond, "Families of the Handicapped Child," 59.

5. Florence W. Kaslow, "Profile of the Healthy Family," *Interaction* 4 (1981):1–15.

6. E. A. Byrne and C. C. Cunningham, "The Effects of Mentally Handicapped Children in Families—A Conceptual Review," *Journal of Child Psychology* 26 (1985):847–64.

7. S. Allen Wilcoxon, "Grandparents and Grandchildren: An Often Neglected Relationship Between Significant Others," *Journal of Counseling and Development* 65 (1987):289–90.

8. Kaslow, "Profile of the Healthy Family," 13.

9. Mary R. Hulnick and H. Ronald Hulnick, "Life's Challenges: Curse or Opportunity? Counseling Families of Persons with Disabilities," *Journal of Counseling and Development* 68 (1989):166–70.

10. Ibid., 167.

11. Ibid., 168.

12. David M. Klein and Reuben Hill, "Determinants of Family Problem-solving Effectiveness," in Wesley R. Burr, Reuben Hill, F. Ivan Nye, Ira L. Reiss, eds., *Contemporary Thoughts About the Family*, vol. I (New York: The Free Press, 1979), 499.

13. Hulnick and Hulnick, "Life Challenges: Curse or Opportunity?" 169.

14. Ibid., 169–70.

Chapter 9. A Faith Perspective: Spiritual Growth

1. George Selig and Alan Arroyo, *Loving Our Differences* (Virginia Beach, Va.: CBN Publishing, 1989), 8, 11.

2. Darlene McRoberts, ed., *Victorious Survivors* (Ormond Beach, Fla.: Logos Light and Life Foundations, 1988).

3. Ibid., Preface.

4. Alan Monat and Richard S. Lazarus, *Stress and Coping*, 2d ed. (New York: Colombia University Press, 1985), 20.

5. David G. Myers, ed., *Psychology*, 2d ed. (New York: Worth Publishers, Inc., 1989), 510–20.

6. Charles F. Stanley, *Forgiveness* (Nashville: Oliver Nelson, 1987); Charles F. Stanley, *Forgiveness: God's Gift Demonstrated* (audio cassette) (Atlanta, Ga.: In Touch Ministries, 1986); David W. Augsburger, *Caring Enough to Forgive* (Ventura, Calif.: Regal Books, 1981); and Lewis Smedes, *Forgive and Forget* (San Francisco: Harper and Row, 1984).

7. Everett L. Worthington, Jr., *When Someone Asks For Help* (Downers Grove, Ill.: InterVarsity Press, 1982); H. Norman Wright, *Self-Talk, Imagery, and Prayer in Counseling* (Waco, Tex.: Word, 1986); William Backus, *Telling the Truth to Troubled People* (Minneapolis: Bethany House, 1983); and Gary Collins, *Christian Counseling* (Waco, Tex.: Word, 1980).

8. J. Sidlow Baxter, *Divine Healing for the Body* (Grand Rapids: Zondervan, 1979); Don Williams, *Signs, Wonders and the Kingdom of God* (Ann Arbor: Servant Press, 1989); Donald A. Carson, *Showing the Spirit: A Theological Exposition of Corinthians 12–14* Grand Rapids: Baker Books, 1987); John Wimber with Kevin Springer, *Power Healing* (San Francisco: Harper & Row, 1987); and Francis MacNutt, *Healing* (Notre Dame: Ave Maria Press, 1974).

9. B. Bonke, P. I. M. Schmitz, F. Verbage, and A. Zwaveling, "Clinical Study of So-Called Unconscious Perception During General Anesthesia," *British Journal of Anesthesia* 58 (1986):957–64.

10. Henri J. M. Nouwen, *The Road to Daybreak* (New York: Doubleday, 1988).

11. Ibid., 19.

12. Ibid., 21.

13. Ibid., 224.

14. Philip Yancey, *Disappointment with God: Three Questions No One Asks Aloud* (Grand Rapids, Mich.: Zondervan, 1988).

Chapter 10. The Church's Ministry to Those with Disabilities

1. David K. Switzer, *Pastoral Care* (Mahwah, N.J.: Paulist Press, 1989), 15–16.

2. Ibid., 16.

3. Allen Johnson, "The Impact of a Challenged Child and Adolescent within the Family: Implications for Support Services," *Journal of Psychology and Christianity* 7 (1988):32–42.

4. Stanley Huerwas,"Suffering the Retarded: Should We Prevent Retardation?" in Paul R. Dokecki and Richard M. Zaner, eds., *Ethics of Dealing with Persons with Severe Handicaps* (Baltimore, Md.: Paul H. Brookes, 1986): 68.

5. Ibid.

6. Jean Vanier, *Community and Growth* (New York: Paulist Press, 1979), 112.

7. Paul Schmolling, Jr., Merril Youkeles, William R. Burger, *Human Services in Contemporary America,* 2d ed., (Pacific Grove, Calif.: Brooks/Cole, 1989): 93-95.

8. Joni Eareckson Tada, keynote speech at the International Congress in Christian Counseling, Atlanta, Ga., 13 November 1988.

INDEX

Rosemarie S. Cook, Ph.D

Rosemarie Scotti Cook is assistant professor in the School of Counseling and Family Services, Regent University, and adjunct member of the faculty of Old Dominion University. Formerly she was a prevention specialist with Mental Retardation Services in Norfolk, Virginia. Dr. Cook holds the B.S. in education from Duquesne University, the M.A. degree in counseling from Regent University, and the Ph.D. in Urban Services from Old Dominion University. She is the mother of four sons: James, Christopher, Steven, and Shawn.